Your Local Government

DONALD C. ROWAT

Your Local Government

A Sketch of the Municipal System in Canada

Macmillan of Canada
Toronto

First published 1955
Reprinted 1962, 1965, 1968
Second edition 1975

ISBN 0-7705-1292-5

Printed in Canada
for The Macmillan Company of Canada Limited
70 Bond Street, Toronto M5B 1X3

"A nation may establish a system of free government, but without municipal institutions it cannot have the spirit of liberty."

de Tocqueville

Contents

Preface to the Second Edition

It is gratifying to know that there is still a demand for a book written twenty years ago. Indeed, the book has remained in such demand that the publisher has never insisted that I should revise and update it. This is partly because, sad to say, many of the reforms proposed in the book have not as yet been acted upon, so that they are still as fresh and relevant today as they were then.

It is true that the main reform proposed—the creation of a second tier of regional local government — has been taken up by the three largest provinces in very recent years. Much of the revision in the second edition is devoted to describing the resulting structural reorganization: the creation of second-tier metropolitan governments in Ontario and Quebec, and the institution of province-wide regional government in British Columbia. But the other provinces have not yet recognized that regional government is needed to prevent centralization at the provincial level and to keep local government strong. Hence, the basic structure of the book still remains sound, and a major revision was not required.

On the other hand, many minor changes have come along in the last twenty years, and it was necessary to take account of these. The book has therefore been completely updated, incorporating changes to the end of 1974. New financial figures are given, new trends are described, and a new table has been added giving the most recent information available on the numbers and types of municipalities in Canada.

As mentioned in the Introduction to the first edition, it is difficult to make brief generalized statements about ten different municipal systems with complete accuracy. And it is almost impossible for a single scholar to keep himself informed about minor changes in these systems. It is therefore likely that a few statements which no longer hold true have crept into the new edition. I would be glad to have alert readers draw any of these to my attention.

For informing me of many such minor changes requiring revision, I should like to thank officials of the provincial Departments of Municipal Affairs, and in particular John R. Cameron, Director of Research for Nova Scotia's Department, whose efforts on my behalf went far beyond the call of duty. I should similarly like to thank my fellow scholars, Jane Jenson, Louise Quesnel-Ouellet, Tom Plunkett, Hugh Whalen, and George Neuspiel (who was my consultant on changes in the local administration of justice), and also Graham Marr of Statistics Canada (who provided up-to-date figures in advance of their normal publication date).

The original objective of the book — to provide a brief discussion of local government and its problems in a readable style for high school students, new councillors, and indeed any interested citizen — seems to have stood the test of time. In fact, it is still the only book of this nature on local government in Canada. Now that it has been revised and updated, university students, too, may find it useful as a brief introduction to the subject, especially in introductory courses on Canadian government. I take the liberty of referring those who want a more sophisticated treatment to my longer book, *The Canadian Municipal System*.

D.C.R.
Ottawa,
January, 1975

Introduction

Today it is essential that citizens and local officials take an intelligent interest in all aspects of local government. They must know not only what it is, how it works and what it does, but also why it is here. If they understand this, they are in a position to know its value to them as citizens or as citizens' representatives.

Perhaps some parts of local government are no longer useful — are merely hang-overs from the past. The reasons for their existence, while they may have been good in their time, may no longer be sound. Perhaps the things which local governments should do for the citizen are so different today from those of the past that the old local governments, because of their size and nature, can't do them properly. If you and I go on demanding those things, at the same time refusing to admit that local government is falling down on the job, then either they will be done badly or they will be done by the senior levels of government.

What we as citizens must do, then, is find out whether this is true. If it is, then we must decide, first, what things local government can do best, and, second, whether the value of local government to us is important enough for us to be willing to reorganize it so that it *can* do these things — and do them well. Otherwise the decision will go by default.

Both the strength and the weakness of democratic local government is its stability. This means that any arbitrary control from above will be met with a healthy resistance. But, unfortunately, it also implies an unhealthy resistance to change of any kind. Too often local citizens and officials — through no fault of their own — lack the necessary stimulants to thinking which would make them see the need for change. Lack of background knowledge and lack of contacts with the changing times are probably the two chief offenders. Lack of interest in the wider problems of local government is another.

This brief book, then, is aimed at stirring up an awareness of these "lacks" by providing a bit of background knowledge on what local government is and how it works, and — more important — by raising questions all along the way. These, it is hoped, will set you to thinking about the many problems that must be solved if we are to answer the most important question of all about local government: Can democracy be kept at home?

In a book of this nature, which attempts to describe briefly and simply what amounts to ten different municipal systems, it is difficult to avoid inaccuracies. Therefore, I hope that I may be pardoned for any that appear. If errors are discovered, I would be glad to have them drawn to my attention. For the removal of many that might otherwise have crept in, I am indebted to Mr. Eric Hardy and Mr. George Hougham of the Citizens Research Institute of Canada, and to Mr. George Mooney and Mr. Tom Plunkett of the Canadian Federation of Mayors and Municipalities.

D.C.R.
December, 1954

1. Where Did It Come From?

Relatively Young

What many people today forget about our present scheme of local self-government is that it is not very old. It is true that some cities in Eastern Canada have long histories of self-rule. But province-wide systems were not created until after responsible government had been fought for and won at the higher levels of government, near the middle of the last century. Indeed, in the Maritimes and the West, municipal government is relatively young. Although locally elected Councils existed here and there in these regions, over-all systems were not created until long after Confederation had been achieved in 1867, and in some provinces large sections of the province still are municipally unorganized.

Despite the youth of these systems, however, the historical background of their origin is long and complex. To the question, ''Where did local government in Canada come from?'' then, even the simplest answer would have to be in two parts, one geographical and the other political. Thus, the answer might be: (1) from England, the United States and right here at home; and (2) from above (the plans laid by senior governments) and from below (the wishes and needs of the local people). The part from above came mostly from here and from England, and the part from below, mostly from here and from the United States.

This, of course, is a much oversimplified explanation, and to understand it more fully we must look more closely into the story of the rise and growth of local self-government in this country.

THE OLD SYSTEM

Naturally, wherever local communities exist within a larger one, ways must be found of controlling them so that they interfere neither with each other nor with the interests of the whole. This can be done—and is done under modern democratic government—by leaving citizens free to run their own local affairs within limits which are pretty clearly set down and agreed upon by their representatives in a legislature. But in earlier times, before this agreement on what the local people should do for themselves, it was much simpler to have them ruled by the central government alone.

This was the way in which the King's representatives and their Executive Councils controlled the local communities in the colonies of British North America before the days of responsible government. The old system, patterned on ancient practices developed in England over the centuries, had become transplanted — root, tree and branch — to the colonies.

Government by Session

What, then, was this old system? Briefly, it was *Government by Session*. This means that the local communities were controlled by appointees of the central government—magistrates who met in legal Sessions. A group of Justices of the Peace for each County would meet in regular session once a year in January (which is why many rural Councils today meet in January); and if a second session was needed, they would meet again in early summer (as with extra rural Council meetings today). At these so-called Quarter Sessions, besides hearing legal cases, the Justices conducted all the necessary business of local government. And they were the only ones who had any real local power. They were chosen from the wealthy landowners, merchants and lawyers. They stood for the King's government. They, and they alone, were there to see that things were done according to law.

But didn't the local citizens have a say? Well, they had some. At each Session the Justices had a Grand Jury to assist them. This Grand Jury was selected periodically from the lesser landowners and others. But it had no executive power. It could not decide anything. It was expected to do two things: first, to present a statement of the expenses required for the support of the poor, the upkeep of the jail and the payment of local officials; and second, to present the names of two persons for every office to be filled by the Court of Sessions. The Grand Jury could also present petitions.

It was the Justices of the Court, however, who made all the decisions. They made local regulations concerning straying animals, pounds, fires, bush-burning and timber driving. They licensed tavern-keepers, and controlled inland fisheries, ferries, wharves, bridges and roads. And they regulated the marketing and inspection of such things as bread, salt, coal, hay, iron and lumber. They also appointed the officials and had charge of the jail, the workhouse and the police.

Session Records

The records of these Courts give a vivid picture of the times. For instance, the records of the Quarter Sessions held at Pictou, Nova Scotia, reveal that in 1811 one Alexander McIntosh was committed to jail on a charge of murder. But the jail was in such a state of disrepair that a special meeting of Sessions had to be called to appoint two armed men to guard the prisoner. It also appears that to discourage trespass by horses the Court had ordered a reward of five shillings to anyone who caught a stray horse and took him to the pound. In February, 1811, the Court withdrew these payments on the grounds that "they were a temptation to anyone in need of a dollar to take up a horse"!

A wonderful variety of business was conducted by these Courts. Take, for instance, the Session for the County of Cumberland, Nova Scotia, which met more than 125 years ago, "on the first Tuesday in January", 1847, in the Court-house at Amherst. Fortunately, the Justices had a Court-house by that time. Some of the earlier minutes contain records of payments to Mr. A. "for the use of his house to hold Court", and to Mr. B. "for the use of his tavern to hold Court". At any rate, there they met, with Mr. Justice McFarlane as President and twenty Justices of the Peace in attendance.

The record states that the sitting began with the usual Proclamation of opening. The Grand Jury was then called and sworn, and from it nine committees were formed to bring in reports. It was on the basis of those reports that the business of the Court was conducted. Then the Court granted several petitions from private persons requesting that they be allowed to do their statutory (legally required) road work on their own property. It ordered that the County boundaries be surveyed and fixed, and appointed one James McNabb to do the job. It renewed the ferry licence of Robert McNutt and Maurice Welsh at Pugwash on condition that they would not put up the fares. It decided on petition from John Chapman of Amherst that he had been overtaxed on the rate for the support of the poor, and ordered a repayment.

Next, a committee of the Grand Jury reported that the law regarding stray geese need not be put into force anywhere in the County except at Parrsboro. The Court thereupon laid down in detail the limits within which the law was to apply. It ordered that all stray geese found within these limits be impounded and released only after payment of expenses and a fine of 2d. per goose—one half to go to the pound-keeper, and the other to the person impounding the goose. The Court then levied certain fines and adjourned till next day.

The first business next day was to authorize the payment of the clerk, auditors, surveyors and others. Tavern licences were granted and the accounts were presented for approval. On subsequent days the Court completed its review of the accounts, and appointed the officers of local government for the County — surveyors of highways, supervisors of roads, overseers of the poor, collectors of taxes, assessors, constables, pound-keepers, hog-reevers, fence-viewers, etc. Finally, their business still not complete, the Justices adjourned, to meet again in May.

The General Picture

This, then, is a picture of how local government was conducted in the colonies of British North America for well over a hundred years. The general impression conveyed by the earliest records is of an orderly, agreeable conduct of business. Most of the petitions seem to have been granted. If there were quarrels between the Justices of the Peace and the Grand Juries, the minutes do not record them. Indeed, one contemporary remarked in praise of the system that the magistrates ''were all men of education and refinement, and their gentlemanly deportment and dignified manner induced a high respect for the bench, and gave a tone of order and refinement to society.''

Yet the whole scheme of Government by Session was contrary to modern principles of local self-government. For it emphasized government from above, rather than from below. As might have been expected, abuses crept in. Although people paid large amounts in local taxes, they had no control over those who levied the taxes and spent the money. While the Justices were usually from the local areas that they served, they were appointed by the governing groups, who naturally had their favourites. Even Justices "of education and refinement" often did not appreciate the common man's needs and desires. And as the population grew and spread, requiring more appointments, it became increasingly hard to find such Justices. Where the governing groups could find no one to fit *their* ideas of education and refinement, they delayed making appointments, sometimes indefinitely. As a result, not only the quality but also the number of Justices became inadequate. In Upper Canada (now Ontario) the situation became so bad that in many areas the business of local government was simply left undone. It is small wonder, then, that the pressure for reform became strongest in this colony.

But there was another and different stream of tradition under the old system which must not be overlooked. This was the ancient British tradition of freedom out of which our modern democracy grew. One aspect of it was the freedom of self-rule granted by Royal Charter in early times to certain towns. Another was a form of rural self-government which had grown up in England through the centuries, and which was the ancestor of the township in New England and Ontario, and of the parish in Quebec.

It had been the ancient custom of church wardens to call together the inhabitants of a church parish in periodic meetings to look after local affairs and to levy rates on themselves for the support of certain services. In the days of Queen Elizabeth these parishes were made units of government for road-building and support of the poor. Later, when other local services were added, such as schools, the money was raised in the same manner—by these *vestries*, or meetings of parishioners. This, then, is the precedent for the local ratepayers' meeting of today, and for the rates to support schools and the poor that are still levied in small districts, parishes, or townships.

The Township Moves In

Aside from this early British tradition, one of the most persistent influences working against the scheme of Government by Session was the American origin of a great section of the people. Even before the American Revolution of 1776, the colonies of New England had contributed over half of Nova Scotia's population, which was about 13,000. New Englanders were all for no interference from outside, and the earliest settlers came only after they had been promised local self-government.

These were the families who moved into Nova Scotia's Annapolis Valley in 1760. They brought with them the tradition of the township and its local town meeting. They were accustomed to electing their own officers and managing their own affairs, and when they arrived in the Valley they didn't waste any time. They elected lot layers, and began laying out lots and "streets" on the land that had been granted them. In King's County today one finds reminders of their work — the roads still called streets, and the Town Plot near Port Williams originally intended for a Town Hall and jail.

The later history of this area reveals many examples of protest petitions, extra-legal town meetings, and special agreements with local magistrates designed to give local ratepayers at least some control of their own affairs. But the conservative Act of 1765 refused the establishment of independent townships and reaffirmed Government by Session.

Although the years just after the American Revolution saw a tremendous influx of about 35,000 Loyalist refugees into the Maritimes, the supporters of the township never did succeed in getting it set up as an independent, self-governing unit, as they did in Ontario, Quebec and the prairies. The impact of the Loyalist immigration was great enough to result in the creation of New Brunswick as a separate colony in 1784. And it wasn't by accident that Saint John was granted self-government the very next year — almost fifty years before any other city in Canada. But apparently the new spirit of independence was not strong enough to break the grip of the old system.

One reason may have been that many of these Loyalists had come from the southern American colonies, where they had already been accustomed to local government by Quarter Sessions. But no doubt the main reason was that the British authorities remembered the strong influence that the town meetings of Boston had had in encouraging a spirit of rebellion. They were therefore determined to stifle the creation of such doubtful institutions in the colonies that had remained loyal. In any case, not until difficulties over arbitrary control had arisen in the middle of the next century did the leaven of democratic thought from the American Revolution take hold in the Maritimes. It was only then that the taste for democratic control of local affairs became sharp enough to challenge the old system seriously.

Although several thousand New England Loyalists migrated into Lower Canada (now Quebec), here too their influence was not great enough to disturb the old system. Indeed, as one official wrote to the British Colonial Secretary about the Vermonters who had moved into the Eastern Townships with their municipal institutions, ''When the impropriety of electing their own officers was pointed out to them, they had quietly given up [these institutions] and promised to conform to those of Canada.''

The 10,000 or more New Englanders who settled around Kingston, along the north shore of Lake Ontario and in the Niagara peninsula, were not quite so quiet. Their pressure was great enough to cause the creation of the new province of Upper Canada in 1791. And within two years they had secured approval for a system of parish and township meetings to elect local officers. Though the powers of these meetings were limited and their officers were still responsible to the Justices of the Peace, the basis for Ontario's later township government had been laid. Not long after, in 1816, provision was made for the local election of school trustees in any section where there were twenty prospective pupils. Despite these advances, however, the Court of Quarter Sessions was to remain the centre of municipal affairs in Upper Canada, as in the rest of British North America, for many years to come.

THE CREATION OF THE NEW

The first real inroads upon the system of Government by Session were made by the towns. As might have been expected, the first towns in Canada to be granted self-rule, aside from Saint John, New Brunswick, were those in Ontario in which the New Englanders had settled. In the years 1832 to 1834 no fewer than six towns — Brockville, Hamilton, Cornwall, Port Hope, Prescott and Belleville — were provided with locally elected Councils, called Boards of Police, to whom were transferred powers previously held by the magistrates. And in the years that followed, towns and cities were incorporated with even more extensive powers — Toronto in 1834, Kingston in 1838, and London, Brantford and Bytown (now Ottawa) in 1847. In the province of Quebec, although Montreal and Quebec were granted self-government on an experimental basis between 1832 and 1836, they were not given permanent Charters until 1840. In the Maritimes, the towns were very slow in obtaining self-government. Aside from Saint John, the only one to succeed in doing so before the winning of responsible government was Halifax, in 1841.

The Thunder Roared

The circumstances surrounding Halifax's incorporation are instructive, for they led to a questioning not only of Government by Session but of the whole system of arbitrary control which it represented.

It appears that for some years the way in which the Court for the town and County of Halifax had been conducting its business was anything but satisfactory. And the local Grand Jury not unnaturally resented its own helplessness to remedy the situation. Finally, it sent a memorial to the Lieutenant-Governor, pointing out that the confusion and obscurity of the financial accounts made its yearly examination of them a mere mockery, and that a thorough reform was necessary. But nothing was done. It then decided to publish the memorial in the newspaper. In January, 1835, Joseph Howe, publisher of the *Nova Scotian* and a great reformer, publicly charged the Magistrates of Halifax with misconduct and corruption. Then followed Howe's famous trial on a charge of criminal libel— and his triumphant acquittal.

These developments magnified the early rumblings of discontent with irresponsible rule by the province's Executive Council into a roaring thunder. Spreading from the arena of local affairs to the wider field of provincial politics, the struggle became transformed into a fight for a government responsible to the Legislative Assembly. This fight, as every Nova Scotian knows, was finally won in 1848.

But what, meanwhile, had been the result at the local level of government? Strangely enough, although the thunder had originally rumbled over the maladministration of local affairs, the lightning did not destroy the old system. The only local place it struck was where the storm had first started: in 1841 Halifax did manage to win a Charter under which it could govern certain of its own affairs. But an attempt in 1842 to introduce a general municipal system modelled on that in the Canadas was discouraged by the British Colonial Secretary.

But the Storm Died Away

Otherwise, Government by Session in the Maritimes went on relatively undisturbed for almost forty years more. Apparently the storm of discontent that resulted in the winning of responsible government had died away after the most important cause of arbitrary control — the irresponsible Executive Council—had been removed. It is true that later a few towns, including Fredericton in 1848 and Moncton, Charlottetown and Sydney in 1855, won special Acts of incorporation from their Legislatures. But, from this time on, attempts to set up a general system of municipal government in the Maritimes were to come as much from above as below, and were to favour the large British County rather than the small New England township.

Between 1854 and 1856, for example, Acts were passed by the Legislatures of Nova Scotia and New Brunswick permitting the voluntary incorporation of Counties by local majority vote. These schemes gave much the same powers to County Councils as Nova Scotia's rural municipalities have today. Yet they were not popular. In the next twenty years only four Counties in New Brunswick set up self-government. Only one did so in Nova Scotia, and within a year or two reverted by vote to the old system. Similarly, an Act of 1856 in Nova Scotia permitting the creation of self-governing townships was ignored by local residents. Finally, in 1877 in New Brunswick, and two years later in Nova Scotia, the incorporation of Counties was made compulsory, and the old system was at last swept away. Altered only slightly by later general Acts governing towns, the systems created at that time in these provinces remained unchanged until New Brunswick's was reorganized in 1966.

As for the other Maritime provinces, Prince Edward Island passed a general Act covering towns and villages in 1870, but never did create a system of rural governments (other than locally elected School Boards). Aside from granting self-rule to St. John's in 1902, Newfoundland did not incorporate local units until after 1937, and not in large numbers until after confederation with Canada in 1949. Almost all of the rural area in that province is still municipally unorganized.

A Unique Combination

In contrast with the Maritimes, the creation of the new system in Ontario and Quebec came much earlier and was closely associated with the winning of responsible government. It was also much more comprehensive, and resulted in a unique combination of the County and the township.

Although in 1835 the famous reformer, Alexander Mackenzie, had won increased powers for township meetings in Upper Canada, the first real break with the old system came in 1840 and 1841, when provision was made for locally elected District Councils in both Lower and Upper Canada. These replaced the Quarter Sessions in both provinces. But they also replaced the local township government in Upper Canada. The new scheme was too centralized, and the Districts were too large. The resulting dissatisfaction led to considerable experimentation in the years that followed. Thus in Lower Canada the scheme was replaced in 1845 by parish and township government, but this in turn was replaced by County government in 1847.

Finally, in 1849, that great champion of self-government, Robert Baldwin, secured the passage of a general law establishing a comprehensive system of municipal government for Upper Canada. This reduced the District units to County size and at the same time reintroduced township government. It also provided for the self-government of all urban areas—cities, towns and villages. Thus Upper Canada had at last successfully combined the British and New England traditions by creating a two-tier system of local government—with Counties above, and townships, towns and villages below, the heads of the local Councils forming the County Councils. It had also succeeded in providing the local governments with wide powers and much freedom from central control. Lower Canada soon followed suit in 1855 with a general Act adding Councils below the Counties, in parishes, townships, towns and villages. Although established over 120 years ago, these are the systems that exist in Ontario and Quebec today, except for the recent creation of metropolitan governments.

Taken For Granted

The prairie provinces, of course, were not created until after Confederation. By this time the principle of self-government had become so well accepted that it was almost taken for granted municipal institutions would be set up. A large proportion of the new prairie population had come from Ontario, and the system created by the Baldwin Act of 1849 had been so complete and so successful that it had a profound effect upon thinking in the West.

Only three years after Manitoba's creation in 1870, for example,

Winnipeg was granted self-rule, and provision was made for the voluntary incorporation of other municipalities. Between 1883 and 1886 Manitoba experimented with a County system modelled on that of Ontario but found it unworkable because of the sparse settlement and the difficulty of travel. The Counties were therefore abandoned, although the local units were retained. Finally, a general Municipal Act in 1902, providing for cities, towns, villages and rural municipalities, established the system that exists today.

Although Saskatchewan and Alberta were not made separate provinces until 1905, the government of the old North West Territories had already set up municipal institutions in these areas. In 1883 and 1884, it provided for the voluntary creation of urban and rural municipalities resembling those in Ontario. Regina and Moose Jaw at once secured local Councils, but the scheme for rural units was too elaborate for this sparsely settled region and few areas took advantage of its provisions. Meanwhile, the government had by 1897 organized the rest of the settled area into numerous small townships (six square miles in area), each with a locally elected Overseer. In that year the Territories were granted responsible government and the new Assembly immediately provided the townships with local Councils. But again it was found that the Ontario tradition had been followed too closely. The township units were much too small for a thin population. In 1903 the rural units were therefore increased in size to cover four townships each.

This, then, was the municipal system that Saskatchewan and Alberta inherited in 1905. The new provinces soon passed general Acts consolidating the earlier provisions for self-government in towns and villages. But as the population grew and spread, it was again found that the rural units were too small. Between 1908 and 1913 Saskatchewan increased their size to nine townships, and beginning in 1912 Alberta did the same. Alberta once more doubled the size of its rural municipalities between 1942 and 1944. It then transferred the powers of school boards to most of them, and confusingly renamed these consolidated units "counties", even though they are not second-tier Counties as in Central Canada. Except for these changes, the municipal systems created earlier in these provinces are basically the same as those that exist today.

British Columbia, too, was influenced by Ontario's example. Even before British Columbia entered Confederation in 1871, a few municipalities, including New Westminster (1860) and Victoria (1862), had already been set up. In 1872 a general Act made provision for the voluntary creation of local units. Vancouver was incorporated by special legislation in 1886, and in 1892 the general Act was rewritten, with provisions for cities and rural units modelled on those of Ontario. As in the prairies, the County system was not adopted, even though it had worked well in Ontario and Quebec. Moreover, villages were not created until much later, and towns, oddly enough, were not provided for until a few years ago.

Compulsory Self-Government

Looking back now, one of the peculiar things about the creation of province-wide municipal systems is that self-government for the rural areas was made compulsory. It was to a large extent forced on them from above, and was often stoutly opposed. How did it happen that the movement for rural self-government came not from the local communities but from above? And why was it opposed?

Well, for one thing local democratic control was everywhere becoming popular, and it was thought that self-government should include all possible areas, even those that did not appreciate its value at the time. During this period England and the United States had been busy setting up local governments on a nation-wide basis. And this no doubt had an influence upon thinking here.

But probably the chief reason self-government was made compulsory — and by the same token, the reason it was opposed — was because it would cost the local ratepayers more. At the time the rural units were created the need for more and better local services, especially roads and bridges, was pressing. And under the new plans the provinces, for lack of adequate revenue, proposed to leave this problem to the newly elected Councils. In other words, self-government was to be a sugar coating for the bitter pill of increased taxes.

Yet the new schemes were successfully introduced and soon became well accepted. Except for the recent abolition of rural municipalities in New Brunswick and the creation of metropolitan or regional governments in the largest provinces, these schemes have remained substantially unchanged to this day. Such durability would seem to indicate that any reasons of momentary political expediency must also have been combined with far-seeing democratic statesmanship. But it may also indicate that the compulsory creation of uniform systems at such a late date, after more than a hundred years of centrally directed Government by Session, did little to sharpen the taste of the local communities for experimenting with future changes. Perhaps they have preferred to let well-enough alone. The structures had hardly been built before the vast social and economic changes of our modern industrial society began to beat against them. So the question we must keep in mind is whether we have not again arrived at a period when major reorganizations are necessary.

2. The Ships of Local Government

Machinery Is Rigid

From Chapter 1 we have learned that early provincial legislation prescribed the basic organization for the system of local government that exists in Canada today. Political scientists are fond of describing such a pattern of organization as the "machinery" of government. And then the citizens and local politicians are said to be the people who run it. The analogy of machinery, however, sounds as though the system were rigid and unalterable—as though the machinery were installed at an early date and couldn't be changed except by scrapping and replacing it. But this is not strictly true. The system *has* changed, even if only very slowly and, in essentials, very slightly.

Besides, the analogy is actually misleading, since local government consists of not a single, uniform, big machine but a multitude and variety of little machines — the municipalities. And considered individually, they are not really like machines at all. Once these structures of local government were built, they became, in a sense, alive. Each assumed a life of its own. They became "institutions"—each a unique collection of customary ways of doing things. In addition to the basic organization set down in the original legislation, each local government has developed traditions that are peculiarly its own. Halifax, for instance, has an unwritten rule that Mayors of Catholic and Protestant religious faiths must alternate every three years. And in Ontario and Quebec, the chairmanship of the County Council is usually rotated year by year so as to secure a representative from each local municipality in turn. Despite the stability of the over-all organization, then, and even though these collections of custom and tradition are always surprisingly persistent, local governments do change, each in its own way.

A more apt analogy may be that local governments in Canada are like ships in provincial fleets. Within a province there are various types and sizes of municipal units, each constructed almost exactly like the others of its type. For purposes of smooth sailing, all have been arranged in a definite pattern in relation to one another within the fleet. And all, under the guidance of their Admiral — the provincial Legislature — have been sailing in much the same direction through historical time. Yet each unit, within these limits, sails its own course and directs its own destiny. Each has its own officers and crew (the municipal Councillors and civic employees), and each has its own passengers (the local citizens) who under our democratic system direct the officers as to what ports they should reach.

What, then, is the nature of these provincial fleets? How many types of municipal ship are there in each fleet, and how many ships of each type? What are their main structural features?

Their Types and Numbers

The system of municipalities in most provinces is made up of four types or classes of local unit — rural municipalities, villages, towns and cities. In three provinces, however, there are no rural municipalities. New Brunswick and P.E.I. have no rural units, and although Newfoundland has some so-called rural districts, they are really towns consisting of two or more settlements. Moreover, Newfoundland and Nova Scotia have no incorporated villages, while P.E.I. had none until after passing a new village Act in 1951. Until recent years British Columbia was unique in having no towns.

It should also be noted that, in all provinces except Nova Scotia, the sparsely settled areas — usually in the north — are not municipally organized. These areas, for the most part divided into Local Improvement Districts, are instead administered directly by the provincial Departments of Municipal Affairs. In British Columbia, as much as twenty-five per cent of the population lived outside organized municipalities until the creation of the regional governments, which now include most of the formerly unorganized areas.

The rural municipalities across Canada have been variously named: "districts" in British Columbia, "districts" and "counties" in Alberta, "rural municipalities" in Saskatchewan and Manitoba, "townships" in Ontario, "townships" and "parishes" in Quebec, and simply "municipalities" in Nova Scotia. Essentially, however, they are much the same, except that those in Nova Scotia are based on the County area rather than the much smaller parish or township. Those on the prairies, especially in Alberta, are also considerably larger than the township.

The chief distinction between the three classes of urban municipality is that cities and towns are larger than villages and their governments therefore have greater powers. Cities, of course, are much larger, and often the powers and structure of a city's government are set out in a special provincial Act, called the city's Charter.

Ontario and Quebec have, in addition to the four typical kinds of local unit, large County municipalities, which are senior to the local municipalities that they contain. Quebec's Counties contain rural and village units, while Ontario's include also towns (except for several "separated" towns). The County Councils are composed of the heads of these local units, except that in Ontario the deputy heads are also included if the number of electors exceeds 1,000, and the towns send, instead of their Mayors, two members of the town Council designated as Reeve and Deputy Reeve. County services are paid for by money collected from the local units in proportion to their total taxable assessments.

Canada's system of local government is unusual in that most towns and cities, and in many cases villages, have been separated from the surrounding countryside. Only B.C., Ontario and Quebec have "second-tier" units of regional or County government which combine rural and urban municipalities. And only British Columbia has achieved a general combining of all urban and rural areas in a second tier of regional governments. In Ontario and Quebec, except for a few of the new metropolitan or regional governments that combine urban and rural municipalities, the cities (and in Quebec the towns, too) are quite separate and distinct from their surrounding Counties and countryside. The pattern in the United States and England is just the reverse. In England the largest cities used to be separate from the Counties, but they were combined with reorganized Counties in 1972.

It is also worth noting that in Canada the legal basis for the system and powers of local units varies from province to province. In Ontario and

New Brunswick the system has been laid down in a single comprehensive piece of legislation, called the Municipal or Municipalities Act. The other provinces, however, have separate Acts either for each type of local municipality or for various combinations of types. Quebec, for instance, has a municipal code governing Counties and their local municipalities and a separate Act covering towns and cities. Four of the provinces, however — Manitoba and the Atlantic provinces other than New Brunswick — have no general legislation governing cities. Instead, they have granted a separate Charter to each city. In Alberta, too, cities had their own Charters until 1952, when a general city Act replaced them. And some of the other provinces have special Charters for their largest cities.

Sometimes, assessment legislation is in the form of sections of the general municipal Acts, as in Manitoba and Saskatchewan. But more frequently it is a separate piece of legislation (except that city Charters usually contain assessment provisions). Municipalities are also regulated directly or indirectly by a wide variety of other provincial Acts, such as those dealing with public health, education, roads and drainage.

A Blurred Distinction

Despite the classification of municipalities in provincial legislation, the distinction between the various classes is not as clear as one might suppose. While the three types of urban municipality have been created to fit differences in the populations of urban centres, there is little uniformity from province to province in the minimum population required for each type. Only five provinces, for instance, have established minimum populations for cities, and these range all the way from a few hundred to 15,000 in Ontario (or 10,000 by special legislation). Ontario and Quebec require a minimum of 2,000 for towns, while Saskatchewan requires only 500. Moreover, most provinces have no requirement for villages and towns to change their status with population growth. So even within a single province, as a result of uneven growth in population, it is quite possible to find villages that are larger than towns, and towns larger than cities. Indeed, some of British Columbia's villages are actually larger than some of her cities!

To increase the confusion, often the distinction between rural and urban municipalities is not clear-cut. The rapid growth of population in the areas surrounding the largest cities in Canada has turned formerly rural units into densely settled communities. These have all the characteristics of towns or cities but are still classed and governed as rural municipalities. Nepean, for instance, a good-sized city which has grown up just outside the boundaries of Ottawa, remains organized as a township.

Such facts indicate that official figures on the number of municipalities of each type should be taken with a grain of salt. Thus Statistics Canada's figures for 1973, the basis for the accompanying table, are not strictly comparable from province to province. Officially and legally, as the table shows, British Columbia had 31 cities—close to the number in Ontario, which has nearly four times the population. But the reason is that B.C. has classed many of its villages and towns as cities.

The table does, however, highlight some interesting information regarding the various types of municipality. Note, for instance, the large number of rural units in Saskatchewan, and of villages in both Saskatchewan and Alberta, relative to population. It also shows clearly the tremendous number of local units in Quebec and Ontario, both provinces together accounting for two-thirds of all the municipalities in Canada. Rather surprisingly, the number of rural units in Canada (over 2,000) nearly equals that of urban units (about 2,100). Adding them together, one finds that the total number of local governments in Canada—even excluding the 143 second-tier regional, County and metropolitan units—now exceeds 4,000.

Too Frail to Sail

Being so numerous, Canada's local units are, for the most part, extremely small in terms of population. Often the smallest are also the poorest in terms of taxable wealth per head. One therefore wonders whether most of them are not, by themselves, too frail to sail the stormy seas of the modern world. Rural municipalities, as we have seen, account for a large number of these units. But even if the rural units were greatly consolidated, there would still be left hundreds of tiny villages and towns that are ill-equipped to provide the local services the modern community requires.

Nova Scotia and New Brunswick earlier tried to meet this problem through special provisions for joint action between adjoining rural and

Municipalities in Canada by type and province, as at Jan. 1, 1973

Type	Nfld	PEI	NS	NB	Que	Ont	Man	Sask	Alta	BC	YT & NWT	Canada
Regional municipalities					75	40				28		143
Metropolitan					3	7						10
Counties and regional districts					72	33				28		133
Unitary municipalities	103	33	65	123	1,590	849	184	786	327	143	7	4,210
Cities	2	1	3	6	68	40[2]	5	11	9	31	3	179
Towns	101	7	38	21	199	149	33	131	102	14	3	798
Villages		25		96	279	141	41	352	168	59	1	1,162
Rural municipalities			24		1,044	519	105	292	48	39		2,071
Quasi-municipalities	171				14		19	9	24		6	243
Total	274	33	65	123	1,665	903	203	795	351	171	13	4,596

[1] Includes urban communities in Quebec, Metropolitan Toronto, and regional municipalities in Ontario.
[2] Includes the five boroughs of Metropolitan Toronto
Source: Local Government Section, Statistics Canada

urban governments. But because of rural-urban friction, especially over the sharing of costs, this form of forced co-operation has not been entirely successful. Another device has been to encourage small urban communities to provide themselves with urban services without incorporation as villages, so that they remain part of the surrounding rural unit for all other purposes. This explains why Nova Scotia has no incorporated villages, and why New Brunswick had so few before its rural units were abolished in 1966.

The three prairie provinces have tackled the problem by creating large special districts for services like education, public health and the provision of hospitals. These districts usually include villages and sometimes towns. But since the districts are different for each service, this has resulted in overlapping boundaries, unco-ordinated services, and increased complexity of local government.

In Ontario and Quebec the problem has been partly solved through the existence of the Counties, which, unlike the special districts, are multipurpose units (i.e., they provide several services on a co-ordinated basis within a single geographic area). Besides their traditional functions, such as the administration of justice and County roads, in Ontario many of these units have taken on other services that require large areas for successful administration, like public health and welfare services.

Metropolitan Reorganization

The inadequacy of small municipalities has become glaringly apparent in Canada's metropolitan areas. A serious problem has been created in nearly all of these areas by the rapid wartime and post-war expansion of population. The urban population has sprawled far beyond the boundaries of the central cities, yet the surrounding municipalities are too small and ill-equipped to handle the problems of this large-scale urban migration. The post-war metropolitan area is a social and economic unit, yet often it has no corresponding unit of local government. Within it, the most important local issues are of area-wide concern, and many services can be supplied most cheaply and efficiently on a metropolitan basis.

In the smaller metropolitan centres this problem was partly solved by having the central city annex the surrounding built-up areas. But in many cases the door was locked after the horse was stolen. In other words, the annexation took place too late—after communities had been built up on a completely unplanned and uncontrolled basis. And in all of the larger metropolitan areas, with the possible exception of Ottawa, the central cities failed completely to expand their borders fast enough to keep pace with the rapid spread of population.

In the Vancouver and Winnipeg areas, the situation was at first eased to some extent by the creation of special metropolitan districts for certain services, such as water supply, sewage disposal, and planning, which obviously require control on an area-wide basis. Greater Montreal had a Protestant School Board, and a Metropolitan Commission to control the finances of the 14 suburban municipalities. But such arrangements for particular metropolitan services left many other area-wide problems unsolved.

In 1953 the urgency of the situation in the Toronto area resulted in the creation of a metropolitan government, the Toronto Metropolitan Council. Like the County Councils, it was made up of representatives from the 13 local municipalities in the metropolitan area. Education was to be supervised by a separate 22-member metropolitan board, and street transportation was to be provided throughout the area by a separate 5-member transit commission. But the Metropolitan Council itself controls most other services of metropolitan-wide interest, including the issue of debentures, metropolitan roads and parks, the metropolitan aspects of sewage and water works, planning and housing, and certain aspects of welfare and justice. As with Counties, costs are levied upon the local municipalities at a uniform rate throughout the area. In 1966 the Ontario government reorganized "Metro" Toronto by consolidating the twelve suburban municipalities into five large cities, called boroughs, and increasing their representation on the Council.

This experiment with a second tier of government was so successful that in 1960 it was copied for the Winnipeg area, which in 1970 was further reorganized into a single "unicity", with only advisory councils in place of the former local governments. In 1969 the Ontario government created a regional government on the Toronto model for Ottawa, and then several more for the whole urban lakeshore complex around Metro Toronto, including Hamilton. In 1970 the Quebec government did likewise for Hull, Montreal and Quebec. Vancouver and Victoria also have a second tier of metropolitan government as part of the new regional system in British Columbia. This means that most large metropolitan areas in Canada now have a metro-wide unit of local government.

The structures or forms of the ships of local government across Canada are, in essentials, remarkably similar. This is partly because whole classes of municipalities have been created by single pieces of provincial legislation. But not entirely. As we have seen, there are several types of municipality in each province, and the legislation varies from province to province. It is rather that much the same philosophy and tradition have formed the background for the creation of municipalities in each province. All provinces have been impressed with the democratic idea that local citizens should run their own affairs, and all have been influenced by the examples of England and the United States.

This explains why, without exception, municipalities in Canada are self-governing. Local matters are determined and local services are provided by bodies directly representative of the citizens. It also explains why, with very few exceptions, services are controlled and taxes are collected in each community or area by a *single* authority, the municipal Council. Experience in England and the United States has shown that if local services are controlled by different elected officials or bodies, especially if each has authority over a different area, the result is not only lack of co-ordination, but confusion for the voters. They don't know which of their representatives to blame if things go wrong. They can't "throw the rascals out" at the next election because they don't know which are "the rascals".

In most local communities, it is true, there are bodies other than the municipal Council that run local public services. But ordinarily these bodies are appointed by Council and it is ultimately responsible for what they do. The chief exceptions are School Boards, which in almost every province are elected and therefore directly responsible to the citizens. Many of these boards, moreover, administer education in areas that do not even coincide with municipal boundaries.

Before the war, education in Canada's rural areas was administered by elected boards of trustees in tiny school districts. It is estimated that there were then as many as 24,000 such districts in Canada. Often these units even collected their own taxes. In recent years most provinces have been creating greatly enlarged school divisions, whose boards have either replaced the local school trustees or assumed most of their functions. In the three most westerly provinces, these divisions often include urban centres. Although education taxes are now almost everywhere collected by the municipalities, most of the new units, like the old ones, do not coincide with municipal boundaries.

In rural as in urban areas, then, School Boards are still quite independent of municipal Councils and usually have the power to demand tax funds from Councils for the support of education. This is not the practice in England, where schools are administered directly by the local governments. The Canadian tradition of independent boards is based on the view that education is so important it should be placed in a preferred position. Having it controlled by separate authorities with a special interest in its development means that it does not have to compete on equal terms with other municipal services for the taxpayer's dollar.

The Mayor-Council Form

The vast majority of municipalities in Canada have the Mayor-Council form of Government. This means that the Council has as its Chairman a chief executive officer with special powers. He is also directly elected by general vote and thus represents the whole municipality, while the other members of Council usually represent only districts or wards within the municipal area. This practice has no doubt been imported from the United States, where the election of a powerful chief executive is typical. Some municipalities, however, still follow the English practice, whereby the Chairman of Council is simply chosen by the members from among themselves and has few special powers. Included in this category are the rural municipalities and villages in some provinces, and the second-tier County, regional and metro governments. In Quebec's towns and small cities the method of selecting the Mayor is optional.

Ordinarily the chief executive is called Mayor in urban units and Reeve in rural units. But there are exceptions. In Ontario's villages he is called Reeve rather than Mayor. In Saskatchewan's villages he is Overseer, and in those of New Brunswick and British Columbia he is simply Chairman. In the rural units of Quebec he is called Mayor rather than Reeve, while in those of Nova Scotia, and also in the second-tier Counties, he is known as Warden.

Besides the election of the chief executive as such, another idea imported from the United States is the short term of office for Councillors, particularly in cities. In most Canadian municipalities the term is one or two years, and, in many, the whole Council is elected anew every year or two. In England, on the other hand, Councillors are elected for three years, and their terms overlap, so that one-third retire annually. Before the reorganization of 1972 the Councillors used to choose a number of Aldermen, who served for six years. Many Canadian municipalities, including most of those on the prairies, have followed the English practice of overlapping terms, with a number of Councillors retiring each year. But not many, except in Alberta and Quebec, have adopted the three-year term, and none appoints Aldermen. The term Alderman is used in Canadian cities simply to mean a Councillor elected from a ward.

Canadian municipalities which have followed both the American tradition of short terms and the English practice of overlapping, may well have taken the worst from both worlds. The theory behind this system is that while the short term ensures close accountability to the voters and gives more citizens a chance to participate in government, the overlapping ensures continuity of experience in Council. But this assumes that new Councillors constantly replace old ones. Actually, what we find in most Canadian municipalities is that many Councillors are re-elected year after year. Hence, the overlapping appears to be unnecessary. It may even be harmful, for it probably tends to discourage the proverbial sweep of the new broom. Voters can't, in one fell swoop, replace the whole of a Council in whom they have lost confidence.

As for the short term, it is coming to be realized that Councillors require more than simply an earnest desire to carry out the public will. They must have experience on the job and some feeling of security in office if they are to deal successfully with the complicated problems of modern local government. The trend in both American and Canadian thinking is therefore toward longer terms of office for municipal Councillors.

Nature of Councils

Although the nature of municipal Councils is much the same across Canada, the basis upon which Councillors are elected varies. Generally speaking, election by districts or wards is favoured, especially in the larger municipalities. However, in the villages and small towns, where there is no need to represent sections of the community, all members of

Council are elected at large, by general vote. This system is also required in the parishes and townships of Quebec and Ontario, while in the rural municipalities on the prairies it is optional. It is also used in a number of small cities, and even in a few of the larger ones — for example Vancouver and Sarnia. An argument for its use in large cities is that Council's proper job is to represent the interests of the city as a whole rather than particular sections. Moreover, if there is sectional representation, the Council of a big city tends to become too large to operate efficiently. Vancouver's Council has only eleven members, and Sarnia's has only nine, including the Mayor in both cases.

Aside from special cases such as these, the size of municipal Councils in Canada varies almost directly with the size of the population to be represented. Villages usually have from three to six members; towns, from six to eight; and cities from eight to fifteen. The number on rural Councils tends to be larger where members are elected by districts, as in Nova Scotia, where several Councils have more than 20 members each. The size of the County and metro Councils in Central Canada varies widely according to the number and population of the local municipalities to be represented. Some Councils have more than 30 members. Because of the rapid growth of population in Metro Toronto's boroughs, the membership of the Metro Council was increased in 1966 from 25 to 33, and again in 1975, to 38 members.

Most of the big cities have smaller Councils. Montreal's is the largest, with 55 members. Winnipeg's new Council has 40 members. Ottawa's Council was increased as a result of post-war annexations to 33 members, and for a time was the largest in Canada next to Montreal's. But it was reduced in 1952 and again in 1971, to only 16. Generally, Canada's city Councils are much smaller than those in Britain and Europe, where they are often as big as Legislatures.

Variations on a Theme

Although most Canadian cities have adopted the Mayor-Council system, they have been encouraged by experimentation in the United States to try variations on the basic theme, and even, in the largest cities, to depart from it almost entirely. One variation which has been adopted widely in the United States and which is gaining increasing popularity in Canada is the Council-Manager plan. Typical of this form of government are a

Mayor and small Council, usually elected by general vote, plus a manager or executive director of all civic departments, who is appointed by Council. Among the larger cities in Canada that have adopted this system are: Halifax, Kitchener, Mississauga, Regina, Saint John, Thunder Bay, Victoria, Windsor, and most of the large cities in Quebec.

Another variation, found in Alberta and Saskatchewan, is the use of a Board of Commissioners as the chief administrative body of the city. In most cases (including Calgary, Edmonton and Saskatoon) the Board consists of two or more appointed officers plus the Mayor. Together they supervise all civic departments and make recommendations to Council. This system is much like the Manager plan, especially in the smaller cities, some of which have only one appointed Commissioner.

The largest cities in Ontario and Quebec (including Toronto and Montreal, the two largest in Canada) have departed far from the typical Mayor-Council system. Perhaps the reason is that it has been found difficult to develop a suitable form of self-government for very large cities. If the Council is made big enough to represent all the various sections and interests in such cities, it becomes too big to work efficiently. It can neither plan a co-ordinated programme, make decisions quickly, nor direct the civic departments effectively. Canadian cities have been reluctant to give the power necessary to achieve these objectives to a single chief executive, as has been done under the so-called Strong Mayor plan in some big American cities.

At the senior levels of government, the same difficulty has been met by dividing the government into two distinct but closely related parts — the Legislature and the Cabinet, or as Walter Bagehot described it, the representative part and the efficient part. The Cabinet is a committee, chosen from and supported by a majority in the Legislature, to which is delegated the job of planning the legislative programme and supervising the administrative departments. Ontario and Quebec have established systems for their largest cities that seem to represent approaches toward this Cabinet form.

The Board of Control

Ontario has developed the Board of Control system for most cities above 100,000 in population, including Ottawa, Hamilton, London and most of Metro Toronto's boroughs.[1] Under this system the Mayor and four Controllers make up a Board of Control. They also form part of Council and sit and vote at all Council meetings. The city Council is thus made up of the Mayor, the four Controllers and a number of Aldermen. The members of the Board are elected at large and devote considerable time to their jobs, while the Aldermen represent wards and are only part-time. Hence the Board is in a strong political position relative to the Aldermen.

The Board also has strong executive and legislative powers. It nominates and supervises the heads of all civic departments, awards all contracts, and prepares the annual budget for Council approval. It makes recommendations, its members usually chair Council committees, and in general it supervises the work of Council. In most cases its decisions cannot be reversed, except by a two-thirds vote of Council. And since its members also have a vote in Council, if they are unanimous on a policy it will usually prevail.

This system works with much efficiency, and Ontario's Board of Control cities are among the best governed in Canada. But a frequent complaint of Aldermen is that the tail frequently wags the dog and that the Board is too often arbitrary in its control of Council. In other words, the "representative part" is sacrificed to the "efficient part". This is not entirely true, however, since the Controllers are directly elected. The real difficulty is that, since Controllers and Aldermen are elected on a different basis and represent different interests in the city, conflicts frequently arise between them. Other than having the "efficient part" prevail most of the time, the system provides no really effective way of resolving these conflicts.

The Executive Committee

This difficulty does not arise to the same extent under the Executive Committee system as it has been developed in Montreal and Quebec. Although the position of the Executive Committee (formerly named Administrative Committee in Quebec) is much like that of a Board of Control, it is more closely related to Council. It is not as powerful as a

[1] It is optional for cities under 100,000. Thus Sudbury adopted the Board of Control system. Toronto had a Board of Control until 1969, when it shifted to an Executive Committee.

Board of Control and its members, except for the Mayor, are chosen by the Mayor or Council from among the Councillors. In other words, the "representative part" has been more strongly emphasized.

In Montreal the Committee consists of the Mayor and six Councillors. In Quebec the Mayor is Chairman, while in Montreal the Chairman is chosen by the Mayor, who is only a member ex-officio. Each city also has a chief administrative officer, called the Administrative Secretary in Montreal and the City Manager in Quebec, who works closely with the Committee. His position in Montreal is not as powerful as that of the City Manager in Quebec, because in Montreal the Mayor and the Chairman of the Executive Committee, as well as the Director of Finance, exercise some of the functions that would ordinarily fall to a City Manager.

Most of the new metro governments in Ontario and Quebec also have Executive Committees, but their membership is usually specified, to ensure a balanced representation from the local units. The Executive Committee of Metro Toronto, for instance, consists of the Metro Chairman, the Mayor of each borough and of Toronto, and three of the four other members of Toronto's Executive Committee.

Since Montreal is our largest city the history of its unusual form of government is perhaps worth describing in more detail. Before 1940, Montreal's Council consisted of a Mayor and 35 Councillors. But because of financial and administrative difficulties which had developed during the depression, many felt that the system should be revised so as to increase the representation from the business and non-political elements in the community. In 1940, therefore, the provincial government instituted a system which was unique among cities of the British Commonwealth and North America.

The city's Council was composed of the Mayor, who was elected by general vote, and 99 Councillors. All were chosen for a three-year term and all retired at once. In size and term of office the Council was thus more like a Legislature than a city Council. Even more unusual was the basis for selection of Councillors. The city was divided into eleven wards and from each were elected six Councillors, three by all electors and three by only those who owned property. There were thus 33 elected Councillors of each type. In addition, 33 Councillors were appointed by various business, labour, educational and professional organizations in the city, such as the Board of Trade, the Trades and Labour Council, the universities and the Property Owners' League. This representation of associations was a radical departure from the principle that legislative bodies should be elected directly by the citizens.

Under the new system the powers of the Mayor were severely limited, and he was not even made a member of the powerful Executive Committee (made up of 2 members from each of the 3 types of Councillor). In 1949, however, the provincial government restored many of the mayoral powers and prerogatives.

In 1962 the province finally abolished the special representation of property owners and associations, and created a smaller Council elected by all voters, initially with three members from each of fifteen wards. The Executive Committee was retained, but with the Mayor choosing its members. Thus the Mayor can dominate his Committee, and if he is also the leader of a majority party in the Council, he can pretty well dominate the Council. Unlike a Legislature, which can vote a Premier and his Cabinet out of office, the Council can't remove the Mayor and his Committee if it loses confidence in them.

Why Not a Cabinet?

Neither the Board of Control nor the Executive Committee system, then, seems to provide as good a balance between the need for representation and the need for efficiency as does the Cabinet system of responsible government used by the senior governments. It is worth noting that several of the small provinces, in which the Cabinet system has worked well, are smaller in population than the largest cities in Canada. Indeed, the population of Prince Edward Island (barely 110,000) is less than that of the 15 largest cities, while the population of Montreal (over 1,200,000) exceeds that of any province except British Columbia, Ontario and Quebec. Why, then, has the Cabinet system not been used as the basis for a form of city government?

One reason, perhaps, is that Canadian cities have tended to copy forms of local government developed in the United States. They have been influenced far more than have the higher levels of government by American democratic experiments. In fact, they have been so eager to adopt American methods that they have not always waited to benefit from American mistakes. One such mistake has been to separate and disperse powers rather than to concentrate them in a single body such as a Council or responsible Cabinet.

Another reason, no doubt, is that the Cabinet system implies party government. The Cabinet must be supported in its policies by a majority party in the Legislature (or Council). Yet municipal elections in Canada have been traditionally non-partisan. The strength of this non-partisan tradition is hard to explain, especially in view of Canada's vigorous provincial and national parties and the participation of parties in local elections in England and most parts of the United States. Perhaps the tradition was imported near the end of the last century after the local non-partisan movement in the United States had become strong, but before the party battle had become well established in English local politics. At any rate, there now appears to be a trend in Canada toward greater party participation in city elections. In the largest cities, most candidates now run under the banner of local civic parties, and some are even affiliated with the national parties (though less openly after several Liberal and New Democratic Party candidates were defeated in Toronto's election of 1969).

Some municipal observers are convinced that the introduction of the party battle would stimulate greater interest in local elections, as it seems to have in England and the United States. It would perhaps also encourage a better choice of candidate. A party would choose carefully before it placed its stamp of approval on a candidate, for it would be held responsible as a party for his actions. Its reputation would be tarnished if he turned out to be a swindler or a fool. And parties could use municipal Councils as a valuable training ground for representatives at the higher levels of government. It would seem, then, that the adoption of the Cabinet system for city governments need not necessarily be counted out on this score.

The Cabinet system requires a non-partisan chief executive, such as a Governor-General, who can help to decide who should head the Cabinet when no party leader has a majority in the Legislature. But this need not be a difficulty, for a provincial government could appoint such an officer, possibly from the ranks of the judiciary, just as the federal government appoints the Lieutenant-Governors.

Another objection is that, if the system were used in the largest city in a province, the Cabinet of the city government, supported by a majority of elected representatives in the city Council, might become so powerful as to rival the provincial Cabinet itself. A more important objection is that a difficult situation might arise where a city government represented a political party different from that in power in its province. Although frequently the political stripe of provincial governments is different from that of the central government, this situation is not serious because, under our federal system, the central government cannot easily interfere with them. A province would have more power to discriminate against a city government whose politics it did not like. It would probably think twice before doing so, however, for fear of losing votes in that city at the next election.

In any case, the advantages of the Cabinet system are such that perhaps it would be worth trying out, and taking a chance on these objections. It might even be possible, with further study and experiment, to develop a special municipal form of the Cabinet system that would overcome them.

3. The People Who Sail Them

The Chart and the Compass

It is not easy to say who actually sail the ships of local government. It is clear that the Mayor and local Council, as captain and officers of the crew, decide the detailed course of their particular ship. And the provincial governments no doubt play an important part in determining in a general sort of way where each fleet is headed. But who provides the chart and the compass?

It must be admitted that you and I and every other ''passenger'' in the local community are responsible for doing that. Under democratic government we are supposed to make up our own minds as to the general course that we wish to follow. Since we are all in the same boat we can't go sailing off in all directions at once. Yet it is practically impossible for everyone to agree on *exactly* the same course. Hence, the best that we can hope to do is agree on the port that we wish to reach, and then try to agree as closely as possible on a course. Then, if we elect representatives who we feel will adhere to our general directions, we can safely leave the detailed decisions to them—provided we insist on participating in the big ones.

The Theory in Practice

That is the theory. But in practice many voters find the problem of mapping out a course and striving to get agreement on it too complex. They become discouraged and frustrated by the challenge and hence lose interest in their government. Others just can't be bothered. Some then try to justify this failure to play their part in the democratic process by saying politics is a fraud anyway. This sour-grapes attitude is really a self-accusation. For if we do not take an interest, not only are we not sure who are sailing the ships or where they are going, but we may actually be letting them head for the rocks.

This lack of interest applies particularly to the sphere of local government — exactly where our influence could make itself felt most easily and directly. While in national and provincial elections about three-quarters of the electors cast a vote, most local governments can consider themselves lucky if half the voters turn out. In Montreal and Toronto, the largest cities in Canada, the proportion is nearer a third and at some elections has actually been less than a quarter. Such a situation should put us on guard and bid us to make sure that we are doing all we can to make local democracy work.

Taking an Interest

If, then, you are anxious to take a more active part in charting the course of your local government, the first thing to do is take an interest in nominations. Be sure that someone is nominated who not only has the community's interest at heart, but can also interpret the voters' views by intelligent action. If you have not done this, you can hardly be excused for refusing to vote because the candidates "are all a bunch of boneheads," or "are all out to feather their own nests."

But how can you be sure that you have a vote? The provincial laws on local voting qualifications vary in detail, but if you are 19 or more years old, a Canadian citizen or other British subject, and have resided for over six months in your municipality, you probably have a vote. The Municipal Act in Nova Scotia adds, rather quaintly, "No person shall be disqualified . . . by reason *only* of being a female" — an interesting hang-over from the days before the political emancipation of women. Nearly all of the senior governments have lowered the voting age from 21 to 19 or even 18 in recent years, and this change is now filtering down to the municipalities through amendments to the various municipal Acts.

In one or two provinces in Eastern Canada, the right to vote locally is still related to the ownership or tenancy of property above a certain value. But usually this qualification is so low and so flexible that it includes nearly all owners or tenants and their wives and adult children. However, provinces requiring votes on so-called "money by-laws" — whereby the voters approve or reject proposed loans — restrict the vote to owners. In some provinces incorporated companies as owners may also cast a ballot in elections or only on money by-laws. This means that the agent of a company can vote twice — once for himself and once as the company's representative. Companies and individual owners may even be allowed to vote in every ward in which they own property. Since the payment of taxes as a qualification for voting has long since been abandoned at the higher levels of government, it is doubtful whether such restrictions and provisions as these should still be used in municipal elections.

Secrecy the Keynote

If you have made sure that you have a vote and have checked to see that you are on the voters' list, what procedure must you go through to cast a ballot?

The keynote of this procedure is *secrecy*. The arrangements are laid down in great detail in the law and are practically the same for all elections in Canada. The reason is that elaborate precautions must be taken to make sure that no one can interfere with your right to make a free choice. Early experience with bribery and other corrupt election practices has proved that insistence upon such precautions is by no means uncalled for. During an election, voting is provided for at one or more Polling Booths in each polling district. In most cities, each of the wards is divided into several such districts. The Booth in practice is often in a church or school basement or some private citizen's front room, where in a small curtained compartment you mark your ballot.

Although there are variations in detail from province to province, ordinarily the voting procedure, as prescribed in a typical municipal Elections Act, is as follows. The only persons who may be present with you in the polling room are one voter for each compartment, the Presiding (or Deputy Returning) Officer and his Poll Clerk (who are appointed by the Council), the candidates, and their agents (one for each). The latter act as "scrutineers" in the interest of the candidate to see that the voting is conducted properly. The Presiding Officer has the power to reject anyone not entitled to be present. Also, unusual powers have been given him to prevent any sudden attempt at interference with the voting or any tampering with the ballot boxes. Thus, he can swear in special constables and have imprisoned for the day anyone disturbing the peace and good order at his Polling Booth.

As you enter the room you must declare your name, residence and occupation, whereupon the Poll Clerk certifies your name to be on the list. (In some provinces, if you are otherwise qualified but not on the list, you may be vouched for by an acquaintance who is.) At the same time one of the scrutineers may check your name off his list. In this way he can tell how many of his candidate's supposed supporters have been in to vote. If there is any doubt as to your identity or qualification to vote, one of the scrutineers may require you to take the prescribed oath before the Presiding Officer. You must then swear that you are qualified, that you have not voted in any other polling place and that you have not received or been promised ''any sum of money, office, employment, gift or reward'' in return for your vote.

Marking the "X"

You then receive from the Presiding Officer a ballot paper containing the names of the candidates — one ballot for each office to be filled at that election (e.g., Mayor, and Councillor for your ward) — and you proceed to the voting compartment. The laws provide that while you are there no one else may enter the compartment or be in any position from which he can see how you mark your ballot.

Since so many votes are lost through improper marking, it is worth detailing the exact procedure as laid down in our typical Act. Your mark must be a cross (X), and may be on any part of the ballot paper within the division containing the name of the candidate of your choice. Care should be taken that it is well-centred and clearly in the form of a cross. A mark which edges over one of the lines marking off your candidate or which looks like a ''Y'' might be rejected. And if by mistake you otherwise mark or tear your ballot, it will certainly not be counted. In such a case, however, you may exchange your spoiled ballot for a new one. You must then fold the ballot (each separately if there is more than one) so as to conceal the mark from anyone who may be curious as to how you voted. Then, leaving the compartment, you must ''without delay, and without showing the face of the ballot paper to anyone'' hand it to the Presiding Officer who must ''in the presence of all persons entitled to be present'' deposit it in the proper ballot box before you go. You must then ''forthwith'' leave the polling place.

Added Precautions

As you can see, the law tries hard to make the procedure absolutely fool-proof. At this point, however, you may be tempted to ask, "But what is to prevent a voter putting the ballot in his pocket and slipping a counterfeit one to the Presiding Officer?" Indeed, in the old days this was a favourite trick. Ambitious candidates, or agents who felt that their candidates' talents were too valuable to the public to be smothered in the defeat of an election, would have facsimiles of the ballots printed privately. Then, just so as not to subject the voter to the strenuous exercise of marking his own "X", they would hand these out already marked (for the *right* candidate, of course!) along with small tokens of their appreciation.

Nowadays, however, in addition to a heavy fine for taking ballot papers from polling places, all ballots must be stamped with the official municipal seal. And severe penalties are provided for any officer in charge who permits the printing of excess ballots. Most election laws go even further, and require the Presiding Officer to initial each ballot as it is handed out so that he can be sure the same one is returned.

Unethical Influences

While the actual procedure of voting is thus safeguarded, the law can do little to prevent some of the unethical practices that may be used to influence the voter. It is, of course, a punishable offence to buy votes outright. But what if candidate A's worker, impersonating B's worker, phones B's headquarters for cabs to pick up voters and then gives fictitious addresses, thus tying up B's transportation system? Or what if, impersonating candidate B, he phones voters and so insults them that they immediately rush out to vote against B? And then there is the story of the candidate's agent who, masquerading in a "dry" district as a drunkard, pretends to be soliciting votes for his opposition. These practices may not be prevalent in your locality. But it is just as well to keep one's eyes open.

At the end of the polling day, the Presiding Officer, in the presence of the agents and the polling clerk, opens the boxes and counts the votes. Questionable ballots are examined by the agents, who may express an opinion as to their validity. However, the decision of the Presiding Officer is final unless there is a petition questioning the whole election. The Returning Officer (often the municipal clerk) then totals the returns from each district and declares the candidate with the most votes to be elected — hopefully the candidate of your choice.

Innovations not used much yet in Canada are voting machines and computer ballots. These are designed to eliminate spoiled ballots and counting errors, and they greatly speed up election results. Ottawa experimented successfully with computer ballots in its 1974 election.

COUNCILLORS

Seeking Election

So much for voting. But supposing you prevail upon a friend who has the community's interest at heart to seek election — what then? Well, first you must make sure that he is eligible. To begin with, he must have a vote. But it may surprise you to learn that several kinds of voters are prohibited from becoming Councillors. The object is, of course, to ensure that only responsible, public-spirited persons represent the people. For example, persons who have or are interested in any contract with a local Council, or who have been convicted of certain criminal offences, are automatically barred. Certain official and occupational groups are also usually disqualified, such as municipal employees, members of other Councils, the judiciary, and in some provinces, Members of Parliament. Usually members of a provincial Legislature are not barred. So a Mayor can be an MLA, and in one instance was even the provincial Minister of Municipal Affairs while still Mayor. In Quebec, clergymen are disqualified. Nova Scotia's rural municipalities and towns also exclude habitual drunkards. (The charitable assumption is that this exclusion has not been found necessary for the cities in Nova Scotia!)

Property and Financial Tests

Assuming that your friend does not happen to belong to any of these categories, the most important qualification he must have in addition to being a voter is that of being a financially sound ratepayer whose taxes are paid up. In Nova Scotia's towns, for example, he must have been a ratepayer for at least a year, and to be a Mayor he must have been a ratepayer for three years (before 1968 he had to be a property owner, but now he can be a tenant ratepayer). To be a Councillor in Halifax he must have paid his taxes the previous year. Several provinces have additional regulations to ensure that Mayors and Councillors are in good financial standing. Thus, one who is bankrupt or insolvent may be ineligible until he restores himself to financial grace.

The argument put up in the past for restricting the vote on money by-laws and the office of Councillor to ratepayers is understandable. Property owners are by far the largest contributors to municipal finances and, because they tie their fortunes to a particular community, cannot easily move in the event of financial mismanagement. With the growth of local and educational services in recent years, however, an increasing portion of municipal revenues is coming from the provincial governments. At the same time there is a growing number of citizens who do not own property yet who contribute indirectly to municipal revenues through their work, rent or provincial taxes. Large groups in this category are housewives, tenants and lodgers. They, too, are vulnerable to mismanagement, and hence should be able to vote on money by-laws and be elected.

Then Comes Nomination

If you find that your friend is eligible on all counts, the next step is nomination. The laws require a nomination meeting, or a period during which a paper signed by you and one or two of his other supporters who are qualified to vote, and naming him as a candidate, must be handed to the municipal clerk. To make sure that he is eligible and that his nomination has been completed properly, it would be just as well to check with the clerk.

In some cities and towns, including those in Quebec, he must also produce a nomination deposit (usually $50), which will be returned if he gains a certain proportion (usually a third) of the number of votes for the winning candidate. This interesting requirement is also used in national and provincial elections. Its object is to prevent candidates with little public support from running, since they would make the ballot too long and only confuse the choice between the candidates who really have a chance. A number of municipalities in the United States try to meet the difficulty of long ballots and to achieve a similar result by allowing each voter to number the candidates in order of preference. The candidates with the fewest first choices are then eliminated and the second choices on their ballots are counted for the popular candidates who are left. Otherwise, those who vote for candidates who are not likely to win have no real voice in choosing between those who are.

In any case, having been nominated, your friend then waits anxiously until the hour set for closing nominations, wondering who his opposition candidates will be. If no one else is nominated, he is of course declared elected automatically. Since a would-be candidate will often decline a contest against an incumbent, who will probably be re-elected regardless of his talents, simply because he is better known, acclamations are not uncommon.

The Voters Like It

If, on the other hand, your friend discovers that he has an opponent with whose opinions he disagrees, he can't afford to be modest or retiring. Politics is a battle, and Canadian voters, though they may abhor corrupt practices, do expect candidates to fight fire with fire. They like a man of action. And they like the idea that this is a country where candidates for office *can* freely oppose one another in elections. That is the democratic way. One of the beneficial results of such a contest is to inform the voters on local issues. What your candidate should do, then, is give them his views on these issues, through public meetings, statements to the newspaper, and other forms of public discussion.

He should also line up his friends and supporters into working committees to campaign for him and on election day to see that his voters get to the polls. There are many who must be helped because otherwise it would be inconvenient or impossible for them to vote. Such persons are the ill and the blind, invalids and persons at work. Few municipalities have a provision such as that in federal elections which entitles employees to two hours' time off with pay. Most of them, however, have achieved much the same result by extending their polling day into the early evening. Many, including those in Ontario, also have an advance poll for persons whose jobs will keep them away from home on election day.

There are electors who arc indifferent as to whether or for whom they vote. Others have honest doubts as to the right choice, and it may take very little to tip the scales of their favour. Especially in cities this "floating" or "shifting" vote is large, and may mean all the difference between success or failure in a close election. Although it is unfortunate that this should be so, your help in getting these voters to the polls may be just enough to swing their vote in your candidate's direction.

The Problem of Pay

Let us suppose that through obviously superior qualities as a representative, sheer brilliance as a candidate, and a whirlwind election campaign, your friend walks away with the election. Now the work begins. He must help to sail the ship of local government. This means painstaking study of many important local problems, and much time taken away from his regular job. Although he will usually be paid something for his loss of time, he should not expect a salary equivalent to the importance of the job.

It is true that Councillors' salaries generally have been raised in keeping with the cost of living. Before the war the *maximum* for rural Councillors used to be fixed by provincial laws at about $5 a Council-day or $50 a year. Since the war these amounts have of course been raised. But they are still relatively low. One reason for the low annual rates for rural Councillors is that they meet only once or twice a year and their jobs are obviously just part-time. Town and village Councillors, since their services are still regarded as voluntary, are also paid little or nothing.

Especially in cities, where the job of Councillor should be full-time or nearly so, the salaries are far too low to match the responsibilities of the job. An undesirable result of regarding the job as part-time, with only part-time pay, is that salaried professionals and other employees don't run for office. They can't hold their jobs and be Councillors at the same time, yet they can't afford to resign their jobs if they get only part-time pay as Councillors. Hence the candidates are mainly self-employed professionals or businessmen, such as lawyers or insurance and real-estate salesmen, who can easily reduce the time spent on their own jobs, and who also find the publicity valuable to their business. And city Councils get overloaded with this type of Councillor, who is more likely to represent the interests of business and the developers than of the whole community. Gradually, however, it is being realized that a city Councillor's pay must be high enough not only to attract the most capable people away from their own full-time jobs, but also to help give the office the dignity and esteem that it deserves.

4. How They Do What They Do

"GOVERNMENT BY DISCUSSION"

It may not seem that having Council members meet as a group to run things is anything remarkable. We see it every day. All our private clubs and societies have similar governing groups. The reason we are not surprised is that this habit is universal for all social relations in a democracy. Its keynote is "Government by Discussion". Decisions are not made arbitrarily by one man, but only after a question has been thoroughly discussed and a majority of the group agree on what should be done. Once they decide on a thing it is pretty sure to be acceptable since so many different viewpoints have influenced the decision.

The Decision-Making Problem

But anyone who has observed or worked in large committees of any kind also knows how hard it is for groups of that size to get things done satisfactorily — just *because* there are so many viewpoints. This is a universal human experience with any variegated group who try to decide things together. With the hundreds of things that local Councils are increasingly called upon to decide and do, the wonder is that they manage to get anything done at all.

To meet this problem democracies have had to resort to a number of devices to simplify the process of decision-making in large representative bodies. Probably the three most important techniques they have developed, for Legislatures and local Councils alike, are: Leadership, Rules of Procedure, and Committees.

The Leadership Technique

Leadership in a Council is provided by the Mayor, Reeve or Warden, who acts as chairman, guides its discussions and sees that its decisions are carried out. Mayors have much more power than Reeves and Wardens. Even in towns they may have a general power to recommend "such measures as may tend to the improvement" of the community. But in cities they have a whole host of leadership powers. These include the executive power to implement Council decisions, ceremonial duties, and political responsibilities, such as dealing with the provincial government.

Usually Mayors also have the power to call special Council meetings as often as they think necessary, while often in rural municipalities special meetings can only be called by a petition of some of the Council members. This power has become more important in recent years because the activities of Councils are increasing and often the regular meetings demanded by law are not frequent enough. Some city Charters, for example, require only one meeting a month. Yet the work is often so heavy that the Mayor must call meetings once or twice a week.

To prevent a Mayor from abusing this power by refusing to bring up some matter that Council thinks should be talked about, the law also provides that a certain number of Councillors can by petition force him to call a meeting. Often, too, if at any meeting a Mayor refuses to place a question before them, a majority can force a vote on the question. It may then become only a "resolution" of Council (which is not as legally binding as a by-law).

An interesting difference between provinces and even between classes of local government within a province is that in some municipalities, including all those in Ontario, the head of Council has a vote. In others, however, including all those in Quebec, he votes only in case of a tie, when he casts the deciding vote. If the head of Council is regarded only as an impartial chairman, there is something to be said for his abstaining from voting. And from his viewpoint, it certainly is convenient politically not to have to commit himself on controversial issues. But since he must also be looked to for leadership and direction, it seems hard to justify any provisions preventing him from voting.

Rules for the Game

The second technique for getting things done is a very old one. Rules of procedure are based on customs built up through centuries of experience in the British Parliament. Each Council has its own rules of procedure which may be changed by by-law, but basically they are patterned on those used by the provincial Legislatures, which in turn were copied from England. The United States, too, uses very much the same rules in all its governing groups. The reason for this sameness of procedure is that the democratic process of decision-making is like the playing of a complicated game. Without rules which are accepted by everyone with little question, the game could not be played. The people's representatives would spend most of their time arguing about *how* things are to be done instead of deciding what to do. Some rules are considered so important that they are included in the provincial law. It is usually provided, for instance, that a majority of the Council must be present at a meeting for it to conduct any official business, and that all Councillors must be given advance notice of special meetings.

The Council Chopped Up

The third device, which must be used if Councils are at all large and there is much to do, is that of committees. By this means, a Council chops itself up into pieces, into groups which *are* small enough to give intensive study to a problem, and to reach agreement on its solution. Each committee of Council then specializes in a particular field of the Council's activities and holds its own meetings. Here it develops its recommendations, along with its reasons for them, for presentation to the whole Council. The latter, of course, can refuse a recommendation and make its own decision, but since the committee is part of the Council, more often it merely formally approves the proposals of the smaller group.

Each committee also oversees the administration of its activity. In other words, along with the head of Council, committees are responsible for seeing that Council decisions are carried out. The regular "standing" committees on the various municipal services continue year after year. Although appointed anew each year they often contain the same members as the year before. Council may also appoint "special" committees to study and report on particular problems.

Another type of committee is the board or commission. Often the distinction between a board and a commission is that the one regulates while the other actually operates a service — say, a public utility. One way in which they differ from ordinary committees is that they are almost independent of Council. Although usually appointed by the Mayor or Council, they are set up under provincial law and often have the power to make by-laws or regulations of their own. They also usually include several members who are not Councillors—employees of the Council or private citizens who have some knowledge of the field—as with a Town Planning or Library Board. It is said that this type of body is necessary because members of Council are inexpert, change frequently, and may exert influence to gain favours, while some activities require supervision by people with expert knowledge, long experience, and no political axe to grind.

"Government by Committees"?

Most local Councils may legally divide themselves into as many committee "pieces" as they wish. Even where the number of standing committees is fixed by provincial law, Council may appoint as many special committees as it likes. Indeed, one wonders whether, instead of calling the system "Government by Discussion", it would not be more accurate to label it "Government by Committees".

Since committees frequently hold meetings of their own while Council is not in session, they are particularly popular in the rural municipalities. In the first place, rural Councils are large. Also, members must travel long distances. Usually only one or two sessions of the whole Council are held each year (often a regular one in January, which lasts for several weeks, and a special one later, whose length varies with the work at hand). It is therefore not uncommon to find twenty or more standing and special committees of one kind and another, each having about five members. This means that each Council member must sit on five or six different committees.

Yet even in towns and cities, where generally Councils are much smaller and meet much more frequently, a large number of committees is highly favoured. It is not unusual for them to have ten standing committees, and some have as many as fifteen, with perhaps three members each. This means that in a Council of eight, each member sits on about six committees.

Are They Too Popular?

Experts argue that it is not good to have the work of Councils parcelled out to too many committees. They say it may become undemocratic in the sense that important decisions by small groups are only rubber-stamped by a majority of the representatives in Council. Too many committees and boards may also mean that the arrangement of local activities is little better than a broken-up jig-saw picture. No one is responsible for fitting the pieces together. This may cause both overlapping and overlooking, with serious consequences as the work of local government increases in our modern, complicated world. By law, Council meetings are open to the public and are widely reported in the press, while the discussions of boards and committees, although of increasing importance, are often held in private. Too many such bodies are therefore likely to confuse the citizens as to who is responsible for what, and thus to open the way for the old familiar game of "pass the buck".

Some experts say that if Councils were small enough and met often enough they could themselves study, discuss, and make co-ordinated decisions on questions that ordinarily come before committees and boards, while the job of seeing that the decisions are carried out could be handled by a chief executive officer— a Mayor, Executive Director, or Manager— aided by a few top-notch, full-time heads of departments.

This is the sort of neat form of city government that management consulting firms love to recommend. But the trouble is that it doesn't fit the complexity of the real world of city politics or meet democratic requirements. A small Council centralizes power, is easily dominated by business interests, and doesn't represent the great variety of groups found in a large city. A large Council elected from wards gives a chance for more citizens to get to know their Councillors, to participate in elections and to serve on Council. It also allows minorities, which are usually concentrated in particular parts of a city, to elect their own representatives.

THE LEGAL BACKGROUND

Must Be Authorized

In considering how the elected representatives do what they do, it is important to keep in mind that local governments in each province of Canada are the creatures of their provincial Legislature. It has created them, it controls them, and it defines their powers by passing laws. This means that what Councils do, and how they do it, must be authorized.

The power must be found in some Act that the Legislature has passed.

Frequently what they do is mandatory upon them. The Legislature says, "You *must* do this or that". Very often, however, the law is more generous: it says, "You *may* do this or that if you like". This is "permissive" legislation. But if no such permission for an activity can be found in any Act of the Legislature, then ordinarily a Council must not engage in it — unless, of course, it persuades the Legislature to pass an Act to authorize the activity. This shows the importance of Councils knowing exactly what the law says. They must know whether they are acting within their legal rights when they do something. It also explains why Councils always keep solicitors on hand as legal advisers.

Laws Within Laws

The most important things that Councils do, they do by passing By-laws or Ordinances. These are, as the first name suggests, "lesser" laws which apply only to the community that a particular Council represents. They are really "laws within laws", since they give expression to provincial laws by saying in greater detail what they shall be in particular areas. A provincial Act might in effect say, "Councils now have the power to tell children what hours they must stay off the streets". A Council by-law, further defining this, might say, "Children must stay off the streets after 9 p.m.", or perhaps " . . . after 10 p.m.". Thus each Council may have a *different* by-law on the *same* subject, depending on what the local community desires.

This, as you can see, is the foundation of local self-government. The less mandatory and the more permissive the law, the more free choice the local community has, and the closer it approaches home rule. In Canada, cities and towns have more freedom in this respect than other municipalities. Indeed, in some provinces their Councils are given a broad power to pass any by-law they please "for the peace, order, and good government" of the municipality — provided it is not "repugnant to" provincial or federal law. This *general* power to pass local laws is an important distinction between the urban and rural classes of local self-government.

How They Are Passed

Since local citizens must observe by-laws or be penalized, the methods by which by-laws are passed and made public are important. A by-law is usually written up by the local solicitor of the Council with the help of the clerk, but the Councillors must be satisfied that it expresses their wishes clearly and exactly. It must then be formally voted upon at a meeting of Council. In most municipalities this means only a majority vote of those present at any regular meeting.

But for large cities, since the actions of Council are more far-reaching, the provisions are often more elaborate. To begin with, formal actions of Council are sometimes dignified with the name "ordinance", while the words "by-law" and "regulation" denote the less important rules of committees or boards. Although the latter may be passed by a majority of those present at a meeting, by-laws (or ordinances) of Council often must be passed by a majority of *all* members or a majority of those present at *two* regular meetings of Council. These provisions, as you can see, are to ensure sober thought by Councillors and to prevent a temporary majority at any one meeting pushing through an undesirable by-law.

Once by-laws are passed, it is questionable whether they get enough publicity, especially since the Courts say "ignorance of the law is no excuse" for breaking it. Often even the lawyers don't know what the by-laws say on a certain subject because they may have been passed during a period as long as a century, and never collected together in an orderly fashion. Some cities, however, publish a periodic consolidation of their by-laws and provincial Charter in a single volume. Though copies are sold rather than given to any citizen who needs one, this seems like a good approach to the problem. Some provinces also require all new by-laws to be printed and made available to the public for not more than a certain sum per copy. Perhaps important new by-laws should also be published in the newspaper and copies given free to citizens affected by them.

More Local Elbow-Room

In all provinces the Legislature retains some degree of supervisory control over the subject matter of by-laws through its agents, usually the Minister of Municipal Affairs or a special board or commission such as the Ontario Municipal Board. Indeed, Nova Scotia's municipal Acts require all by-laws of town and rural Councils, including amendments and repeals, to be approved by the Minister before they can take effect. Moreover, the Minister has power to revoke his approval at any time and to declare a local by-law no longer in force. He can also veto Halifax's city ordinances (but only within three months after they are passed). In Quebec, as well, municipal by-laws may be disallowed, and in nearly all provinces money by-laws must be approved by a provincial authority.

One reason for this review is the Legislature's desire to make sure that Councils are not acting beyond the powers granted to them. Another is to see that they do not violate the principles of sound public finance and administration. Even though the Legislature may have passed general laws to regulate its local governments, some sort of continuing supervision is needed. Otherwise a local Council might disregard the wider public interest.

The Legislature itself cannot be expected to supervise, for this would mean dealing with individual cases as they arose, and might result in discrimination instead of uniform application of the law to all persons and municipalities. It would certainly lead to a confusion of detailed laws. In any case, local self-government would have no meaning if every action were prescribed by law. So what the Legislature does, then, is to say in only a general way what is to be done and the method of doing it, and to leave the details of supervision to an appropriate, specialized provincial agency. By expanding the area of administrative approval and thus being able to write more general and more permissive laws the Legislature can give more elbow-room to local Councils.

But the wider the authority given to the municipalities, the more urgent it is to see that they keep within the limits intended by the Legislature. Even if Councils do not consciously wish to exceed their powers, new problems are always arising and borderline cases are always coming up in which Councils do not know whether they have the legal power to act. Very often no one — not even the legal adviser — is quite sure exactly what the wording of a particular Act means, or whether the Legislature intended it to cover the activity in question. Words play queer tricks that way. Without some sort of review, the local Council would naturally tend to interpret the meaning to suit itself. Someone who is absolutely impartial is needed to tell the municipalities what activities the general wording of an Act does or does not include, precisely where their powers start and stop.

Where the Courts Come In

Where provincial approval is not required, a good check on possible illegal or arbitrary action by a local Council is the Courts. The most common way in which they enter the picture is for some person (or corporation) who is being injured or compelled by a by-law, to raise the question in court whether it was within the power of the Council to pass it. The Court may then declare the by-law *ultra vires (beyond the power)*, meaning that the Council did not have legal power to pass it and therefore it has no legal force or effect. Or the Court may find that it was validly enacted but is not applicable to the particular circumstances.

England and some provinces in Canada also provide in their municipal Acts for the direct "quashing" of by-laws. This means that private citizens may take a "motion to quash" to the Courts if they think a by-law is illegal or being applied in an illegal manner. Canadian Courts have quashed a number of by-laws in this way, and the reasons they have given are very general indeed—such as "unreasonable", "grossly unjust" or "uncertain". Giving the Courts power to quash on such general terms puts a very broad power in their hands. Yet where there is no Ministerial approval of by-laws, it does help to prevent Councils from exerting any arbitrary control over their citizens.

A by-law is not necessarily legal even though it has been approved by a provincial authority. Since such authorities are, like the municipalities, only agents of the Legislature, their approval of a by-law does not necessarily mean that the local Council had the legal power to pass it—at least, that's what the Courts might say if anyone ever questioned the by-law in a legal action. This, as you can see, is really an added protection for the citizen.

Although the absence of by-law approval gives greater freedom to local Councils, whether it gives the citizen enough freedom from unwise or arbitrary action by Councils is questionable. A by-law is effective *until* it is questioned in Court, and since court cases are so troublesome and costly, some by-laws of questionable legality continue in force simply because private citizens can't afford to challenge them, though some by-laws of this nature are not enforced because the Council, too, doubts their legality.

The Device of Incorporation

Sometimes, even though an action of Council may be legal in the sense that it is authorized by the Legislature, it may adversely affect a particular person or corporation in unfair ways that have not been foreseen. Although provincial agencies can do much to clear the air through their powers of disapproval, so many detailed border-line cases keep arising that they would have neither the time nor the energy to investigate every case. It is here, then, that the Courts do their biggest job of protecting the citizen from injurious action by local Councils.

This has been made possible through the legal "incorporation" of municipalities. By means of this device the municipality and all its inhabitants are considered a legal person—just as a business corporation is — and the Council is its agent. This means that— unlike the higher levels of government which in this sense are above the law — if a municipal corporation is injured by or injures someone, it can sue or be sued in the Courts just like any private citizen.

Negligence and Nuisance

One type of legal liability a municipal corporation may have is for injury to persons or their property through negligence or by the creation of a nuisance. Broadly speaking, however, municipalities are surprisingly free from such liability. The principles of liability are mainly based on decisions of the English Courts, which have drawn a distinction between municipal acts of "nonfeasance" (*not* doing) and of "malfeasance" (*wrong* doing). They say municipalities are liable only for the latter. An act of malfeasance by a municipality is one where its agents have not used the skill or ability that would ordinarily be used by "reasonable" men under the circumstances. Thus, if its employees did not put night lights on a bridge that they were repairing, it might be sued successfully by someone who fell through the bridge. On the other hand, you cannot win a case against a municipality simply because its fire chief didn't succeed in putting out your fire, provided he has done no active wrong. He may have been guilty of *non*feasance; but it was the fire that caused the damage. With nuisance, as with negligence, the only case in which the municipality is likely to be held liable is where the Legislature gives it discretion to act and it causes a nuisance in exercising its discretion—for example, in the placing of a municipal garbage dump.

Having filled in this sketchy background on the *legal* procedures Councils go through, we have now completed our picture of how Councils do what they do. But a picture can never be a substitute for seeing and hearing the real thing. This "atmosphere" can be gained in only one way —by actually sitting in on some of the meetings of your local Council. By law, they are open to anyone who cares to listen and you will no doubt be welcomed. There you will see local democracy at work. If, on the other hand, what you see disturbs or alarms you, the guilty conscience should be yours — because the remedy lies in your hands.

5. What Do They Do?

The "Domestic" Work

Today it is much easier to say what local governments *are* doing than what they *should* be doing. The term "government" brings to many minds the notion of co-ordinating and regulating the activities of society on a wider-than-local scale. Such matters as liberty of the subject, national defence, imports and exports, economic controls, the ownership and inheritance of property, the relationship of husband and wife or employer and worker — all are recognized as the proper concern of provincial or national governments.

What, then, is the chief concern of local authorities? One popular and persuasive answer is that they should do the "domestic" work of a civilized community — keep the place tidy and fit to live in, sweep the streets, see that the houses are properly built, provide cultural facilities for old and young, educate the children, tend the sick, and care for the poor and aged. This sounds like the proper job for local government.

But even if we accept this definition as a guide we run into the ticklish question of just where the local community starts and stops. In the old days it was much easier to draw the line. Difficulties of transport isolated communities and made local organization not only desirable but necessary. Even in the days before the creation of municipalities, because journeys took so long the Sheriffs and Justices of the Peace were appointed from, and partly represented, the local communities. A central department could not have kept in intimate touch with their activities. But now a national or provincial service organized with close control from the centre and reaching out in daily contact with remote areas, is quite possible. Thus today we have federal departments carrying out functions in many localities through their own offices and staff. Examples are the national employment services, the family allowances administration, the income tax offices, and Information Canada.

A second difficulty in defining the job of municipalities is that government nowadays is being asked to do much more than ever before. This again raises the question as to which level of government should take on the work. Though most of it falls into the category of domestic work just mentioned, local authorities find themselves ill-equipped to perform the new jobs. As a result, the public is tempted to take the easiest way out and to ask the higher, more wealthy levels of government to supply the services instead.

THE TRADITIONAL FUNCTIONS

Regulating Conduct

In only one broad field of the traditional *regulatory* functions of government has the division of responsibilities remained fairly clear. Municipalities have always had a good deal to do with regulating the conduct of individuals in order to protect the welfare of the local community. The municipal Acts all contain long lists of the specific kinds of regulation with which Councils may deal, and an important part of their work is control of this kind.

Typical examples for rural municipalities, taken from one of these Acts, are: regulating the firing of guns and the management of log booms to ensure that they are not dangerous to the public safety; restraining the "going at large" of domestic fowls; controlling brush-burning and the cutting of ice on lakes; requiring the removal of snow; "abating all public nuisances"; and licensing "hackmen, waggoners and cartmen". For towns and cities, examples are: regulating halls for "preventing accidents therein"; making building by-laws to ensure that the developer does not have too much his own way; fixing closing hours for shops; licensing restaurants and trades, and gasoline pumps and "swinging sign-boards" to make sure that they are safe and not too unsightly; controlling children "coursing or coasting upon a sled" in busy streets; and preventing "unusual noises" and loitering. All these imply some curbing of freedom in the common interest. And failure to comply with by-laws on these subjects involves legal proceedings and penalties. There may be anywhere from 50 to 100 such subjects listed for rural municipalities. For towns and cities the lists are, of course, much longer.

Even in this field of regulation there have been changes in what Councils may do. Social and economic changes have demanded them. For example, in recent years, to "hackmen, waggoners and cartmen" has probably been added "truckmen", and to the list of licensed games, "automatic machines". Towns and cities have had to be given the power to control parking and to install parking-meters. Yet generally speaking the lists have remained much the same. Few would deny that it is the proper job of local government to go on regulating these "homely" activities which, though often seemingly of no great import, affect the lives of citizens so intimately. Thus each community can regulate itself according to conditions, customs and desires that are peculiarly its own.

In another aspect of the regulatory sphere, however—enforcing the law — there has been an increasing conviction that the municipalities have been saddled with too much responsibility. In many provinces they must maintain courthouses, jails or lock-ups and, besides police, such provincially appointed officers as magistrates, sheriffs and registrars of deeds. The municipalities argue that it is not primarily their job to administer justice—especially since they often do not collect the most lucrative fines from the breaking of provincial laws (e.g., liquor laws). But towns and cities would probably admit that they should maintain their own police, since the latter, besides enforcing by-laws, perform many other local services, like directing traffic.

The Traditional Services

The logical provincial-local division of responsibility has been even hazier with regard to the traditional *services* that local government has provided for its citizens. Chief among these have been the support of the poor, roads, and education. These services have steadily branched out in their wider-than-local aspects, of late even to national proportions.

It is perhaps not surprising that in these areas where there was doubt as to the logical administrator, the services were made *mandatory* for the localities. The chief virtue of the old Poor Laws was that if the provinces didn't look after the poor they at least compelled each community to look after its own. One of the main reasons for creating municipalities was to require them to build and look after the provinces' roads and bridges. The provinces later took over the through roads as provincial highways and assisted with secondary roads. Yet, except in the Maritimes where the provinces look after all rural roads, municipalities still are primarily responsible for roads and urban streets.

The history of education, too, illustrates this same mandatory aspect. When the provinces first made education free and compulsory it was the local ratepayers who were required to bear the cost. Whereas formerly local trustees had been appointed by the provinces, they could now be elected by the ratepayers. Here, as with the creation of the municipalities, local election seems to have been a sort of sugar coating for the bitter pill of obligatory taxes. From then on, despite ever-increasing provincial participation in school administration, the provinces have continued to require the local authorities to make a special levy for school purposes.

Why They Were Local

The main reason local authorities were asked to look after these traditional services was financial. In the days before the modern use of income and corporation taxes, or the growth of gasoline and liquor taxes, next to customs duties the most important single way in which government obtained money to run its affairs was through the general property tax. Here the principle was to have a man contribute to the support of government according to how much property he owned — land, buildings, animals, personal effects, and so on. What governments had to do, therefore, was set a value on or *assess* a man's property in order to know how much tax to charge to him. Since the people who knew best what a man owned and how much it was worth were those who lived in his community, this tax was highly suited to being collected at the local level. This, then, explains why the provinces were tempted to require the municipalities to pay locally through the general property tax for needed improvements to public services like roads and education. After handing control over customs to the new central government in 1867, the provinces had no such great source of taxation themselves.

On the other hand, the property tax, because it was collected *directly* from individuals, and to a large extent *according to their wealth*, was unpopular. It was hard to persuade people to pay for public services in this way. Ratepayers felt that they should get something *directly benefi-*

cial to their property in return for the tax. This explains why the opposition to paying for such services through local taxation has remained strong.

Towns Were More Receptive

There has been a marked difference between the rural and urban areas in this matter of the provinces requiring tax support. It is almost true to say that, in the past, rural governments have been little more than reluctant tax-collecting agencies of the provinces for the support of schools, roads and the poor. Voluntary local self-government has been largely an urban affair. Towns (and later, cities) became incorporated because they *wanted* to, through a majority vote of their ratepayers.

Probably the main reason is that towns were better off than rural municipalities. This meant that a property tax for the support of education or the poor did not have to take away as great a proportion of their wealth to supply the same level of services. Yet even in urban areas there is a continuing reluctance to pay for social services in this way. This helps to explain why the provinces have set up School Boards which are independent of local governments and which have the power to require Councils to levy enough taxes to balance the Boards' budgets.

Another reason why towns were more anxious to govern themselves is that they wanted the services that a civilized urban centre ordinarily requires — such things as police and fire protection, paved streets, sidewalks and street lighting. These could be obtained only by joint effort through a local government. Most of these urban services, moreover, were thought to be directly beneficial to the real property that they served. Hence, it was not hard to persuade local property holders that they should set up a local Council to supply them.

"Public Utility" Services

As urban communities grew, the prosperous cities and large towns in particular found that there were more and more such services with which they could thus supply themselves. For example, it became common for them to own and operate such diverse "public utility" services as water and sewerage systems, garbage collection, ferries, and exhibition grounds. In most provinces urban governments took over the distribution of electric power and the operation of mass transport services. Although these utilities were usually set up under specially incorporated boards or commissions, the latter were usually appointed by the local Councils. In several cases they involved the joint action of two or more municipalities, especially in metropolitan areas.

Some of these experiments in community ownership and inter-municipal co-operation have been notably successful. The Toronto Transit Commission, for example, has an enviable record on this continent, among public and private mass transport systems alike, for its efficiency and service. To safeguard the public interest, the rates and operations of both privately and municipally owned utilities are now commonly regulated by provincial public utility boards.

THE NEW SOCIAL SERVICES

The Positive Approach

Besides these many things that local governments do or may do, recent years have seen a tremendous expansion in that category of "domestic" duties known as social services. In this respect there has been almost a revolution in social thinking. In the old days the dominant idea was that government should only control and regulate the activities of its citizens in the common interest. It was not then realized that the community, through government, could do a host of things to improve the health and welfare of its members that would be impossible to accomplish through individual effort.

Councils are now meeting the challenge of this new idea by trying to make their "home" a happier place in which to live. It is well known that parts of many towns and cities are unsightly and noisy, are crowded and jerry-built, and contain slums which are breeding-grounds for disease, crime and child delinquency. Adult education, public libraries, public concerts and plays, parks and playgrounds, auditoriums, swimming-pools and rinks, traffic police for schools, juvenile courts, day-nurseries, health clinics, housing and slum clearance — all these things and many more are becoming the concern of Councils who wish to improve the cultural, recreational and social environment of their citizens. They are all seemingly the sort of "housekeeping" work that local government might be expected to do.

Planning and Zoning

Part and parcel of this modern development has been a growing consciousness of the need for community planning and zoning. Towns and cities in Canada, partly because they grew so fast, have grown up crazy-quilt fashion, without rhyme or reason. Factories, shops and houses are often jumbled together in a most unhappy, inefficient and even unhealthy way. To help remedy this situation the provinces have been urging municipalities to draw up Master Plans for the future development of their communities, and zoning by-laws which would aim at organizing the towns and cities into separate business, factory and residential zones.

Yet to undo what has been done is one of the slowest and most difficult jobs in the world. Buildings, once erected, last sometimes for a century. It would be a great loss of work and material to tear them down. Besides, they always belong to somebody — a citizen or corporation — whose rights must not be interfered with except for very good reasons. In drawing up its Master Plan, then, a local government must be careful that it is not a pie-in-the-sky plan. Not only must it figure out how its town or city should be laid out for maximum beauty, efficiency and welfare; it must at the same time take into account the existing set-up, its own financial resources and the reasonable prospects for future growth. Otherwise, it might wait forever for the money to implement its grandiose plans.

Planning No Picnic

The whole process of planning is particularly difficult in a democratic community. Ideally, at the time a Plan is developed the local citizens should contribute to its creation and approve of its proposals. Otherwise, though the Plan may be the latest in scientific efficiency, it may be out of touch with local needs and peculiarities. At the same time, since many of the proposals make use of highly technical engineering and other knowledge, the average layman may find it hard to judge their merits.

The usual technique for tackling this difficulty has been to create a Planning Board, made up of qualified citizens, who with the help of one or two technical experts, prepare an official Plan. The Plan is then publicized and exhibited, and any objections to its proposals are considered by the Board. It must then be adopted by the local Council and given official approval by a provincial ministry or agency.

Even after a Plan has been adopted, it still requires to be implemented

— and over a long period of time. In a changing community old Plans often cannot fit new conditions, and new needs must be met in a democratic way. A Plan will have to be changed from time to time and implemented in detail. Who is to be responsible for change and implementation? It is argued that if a local Council were given complete power, it would be likely to abuse the privilege by playing political favourites and making ruinous exceptions in individual cases. The Planning Board is therefore usually retained as adviser to the Council, and any implementation or change requires, if not the Board's approval, at least its published opinion. Yet if part of the responsibility is left in the hands of an appointed Board, it may be out of touch with what the community wants or is willing to pay for, often leading to friction and inaction—especially since the Council may have approved the Plan only very reluctantly in the first place.

Another difficulty in large metropolitan areas is that, while the whole built-up area is a social and economic unit, the job of planning its development may be divided up among the many local governments in the area. And they may all develop little Plans of their own, none of which agrees with another. Although most metropolitan areas now have an overall planning authority—either the metropolitan Council itself or a separate Metropolitan Planning Commission—a single municipality can still ruin a joint Plan by refusing to implement its part of the Plan.

Add to all this the lack of municipal finances for accomplishing many of the things a community would like to include in its Plan—such things as low-rental housing, slum clearance and the removal of buildings to make way for new express routes— and you can see that the process of developing and maintaining a sound Plan is no picnic.

Provincial Pondering

The provincial Legislatures have pondered this problem for over thirty years. It was during World War I that they passed their first Planning Acts. The municipalities, however, did not get very far with the idea. Not many of them appointed Boards and few finalized an actual Plan. During and after World War II, therefore, new Acts were drawn up which, it was hoped, would be more workable. Stirred no doubt by the vitalizing influence of wartime changes, most of the larger cities set up Planning Boards. A survey conducted by the Community Planning Association in 1954 revealed that over three-quarters of the urban units with more than

25,000 population had some kind of Planning Board. But of those between 5,000 and 25,000 only about one-third had Planning Boards. And despite the large urban population in Quebec, such Boards were almost non-existent in that province.

Unfortunately, creating a Planning Board does not in itself represent a record of accomplishment. Not many Planning Boards have been provided with an adequate planning staff, and have succeeded in preparing a suitable Plan. Still fewer urban Councils have approved official Plans and even fewer are managing to overcome all the problems in the way of putting them into effect.

Many students of the subject are now of the opinion that this is partly because the local organization for planning has been wrong. They say it is a mistake to have a separate Board prepare a once-for-all Master Plan. Planning is a continuous process, and the Council itself, advised by its own expert officials who have the day-to-day job of running the government, should take on the job. In this way the traditional gap between a pie-in-the-sky Plan and the grim reality would be closed, and citizen participation would be enhanced.

How Much It Costs

From this brief review of the far-reaching nature of the new social services, it is clear that local government can play a vital role in improving the health, welfare and cultural enjoyment of its citizens. But it can only do this if it is equipped with enough money and the proper tools for the job.

To get a better idea of how much money local Councils spend and of the relative importance of the things they do, let us look at how much their services cost across the whole of Canada in a recent year:

		$ Millions	Per Cent
1.	Education	4,802	47.8
2.	Transportation	1,217	12.1
3.	Health, Welfare and Recreation	997	10.0
4.	Sanitation and Waterworks	864	8.6
5.	Protection (Police and Fire)	706	7.0
6.	Debt Charges	841	8.3
7.	General Administration and Other	619	6.2
	TOTAL	10,046	100.0

This tabulation, based on Statistics Canada estimates for 1972, shows education as by far the most costly of local services, accounting for almost half of the total. But we must note that the money is nearly all spent by independent School Boards over which Councils have little control, and that about half of it is provided by the provincial governments. The tabulation also shows that, because of the post-war population shift to the cities, the other costly services are typically urban: streets, sewers, waterworks, and police and fire protection. In rural areas, roads are the most costly item next to schools.

Health and welfare services have declined in relative importance in recent years, due to the development of programmes which are financed and run entirely by the senior governments. On the other hand, urban recreational and cultural services have expanded, thus maintaining the whole area of social services as one of the most costly.

Debt charges, though by no means small, now account for far less of the total than they did during the depression. They are not a separate ''service'', of course, but it is difficult to discover for which of the other fields of expenditure they are made.

Altogether, local units receive and spend annually on educational and municipal services a total amount of money that now exceeds the impressive figure of ten billion dollars.

6. Those Who Finish the Job

Decision-Making Bodies

What Councils do today, then, is big business. Not only do they help to teach the children and tend the poor and the sick. They build the streets and inspect the buildings. They direct the traffic and help enforce the law. They put out fires, supply water, install sewerage, take away garbage, and remove snow. They regulate shops and administer parks and run utilities and plan whole towns. To do such things they must make contracts and pay salaries and collect taxes.

Many of these jobs require great knowledge and long experience and extensive training if they are to be done efficiently. Law, administration, finance, accounting, statistics, personnel relations, building codes, architecture, safety developments, many types of engineering, social welfare techniques, public health and sanitation, educational methods, scientific assessment— all these things and many more must be known to run the local government of today. Its activities are becoming so extensive and complex that they can no longer be carried out, as they so often used to be, almost single-handed.

Councils therefore must be mostly decision-making bodies. All they can hope to do is plan and decide in a general way what is to be done— and then direct others to finish the job. They must have helpers and advisers, experts and administrators, officers and employees. This chapter, then, is concerned with those who finish the job.

The Age of Experts

In the old days, when the work of local government was simple, it was the custom to call upon local citizens who had some knowledge of an activity to volunteer their services in supervising any job that needed doing. It is still the custom of some rural units to appoint annually for each polling district (on the advice of the Councillor for that district) a bewildering array of citizen-officials—assessors, collectors, electoral officers, sanitary inspectors, "overseers" of the poor, fence viewers, constables, pound-keepers, fire-wardens and what not. As the complexity of municipal work increases, however, it becomes increasingly necessary to have full-time experts in one specialized field after another. A review of the work carried on by Councils today suggests that they need the expert services of: a skilled administrative officer, a treasurer, an accountant, auditors, an engineer, an assessor, a collector, a solicitor, a fire chief, a police chief, a medical officer, a supervisor of welfare, an inspector of buildings, an architect, a personnel officer and a public relations officer. Of course, there are only a few municipalities that can afford to hire a full-time expert in each of these fields.

Full-time Versus Part-time

Fortunately, most local units don't need the services of such experts full-time. They can therefore meet this need for expert assistance in one of two ways. They can either try to hire a separate expert in each field on a part-time basis, or hire persons full-time who can serve as experts in two or more fields. For the smaller units, either method is difficult.

If, however, a municipality has a choice, most students of government agree that the second is the better one. A part-time municipal officer finds himself in the position of serving two masters — the municipality and either himself or someone else. Even if there is little danger of his turning his municipal work to his own advantage, there is always the possibility that he will not carry it out energetically, simply because it is only a part-time interest.

Some provinces have recognized this in their legislation by *requiring* that in the larger municipalities certain jobs, such as solicitor, police chief and assessor, be full-time, and by giving the municipalities permission to appoint one full-time person in place of several part-time ones for a single job (e.g., assessor), or one full-time person to two or more jobs (e.g., clerk and treasurer).

The Clerk-Treasurer, Jack of All Trades

In the smaller municipalities the clerk-treasurer has had to try to meet the need for expert assistance. One person usually holds both jobs and, indeed, is often the *only* permanent paid official available to help to run the Council's day-to-day business. Not only must he act as secretary and treasurer for most committees, boards and commissions. He must also try to be an expert in every field for which the Council has not hired a specialist. Hence, it may not be too much to say that upon his quality more than anything else depends the efficiency of local government in small municipalities today.

"Good Behaviour"

The importance of the jobs of clerk and treasurer are recognized by the fact that they are usually the only municipal appointments that must be permanent. In several provinces, once a clerk or treasurer is hired he holds his job by law during "good behaviour" and cannot be removed or have his salary reduced, except for "cause". In plain English this means his Council cannot fire him or cut his pay except for obvious misconduct in office. Even if it did, he could appeal to the Courts for a decision on whether his action actually did constitute misconduct. In such a case the Judge might say his dismissal or salary reduction was "without due cause", and reinstate him or order his salary to be raised again — especially if the reduction was intended to force him to resign. Even if the Judge's decision went against him, he could further appeal to the provincial Supreme Court.

The Question of Tenure

This raises the important question of how permanent an official's job should be. The old American theory was that the more officials there were, and the more frequently they were changed, the better. This, it was argued, would ensure the active participation in local government of as many citizens as possible, and would prevent permanent officials from dictating to changing elected Councils.

In actual practice, however, especially as the work of municipal Councils grew, having the work so parcelled out meant that it became uncoordinated. No one knew exactly what the officials were doing. Councillors were tempted to appoint their friends to office regardless of their fitness and to expect favours in return. Besides, having the work handled on such a temporary basis meant that it was not performed efficiently. And as the need for expertness and continuity grew, it was seen that a good trained man would not take a job with a local Council if he thought he might be thrown out after the next election or at any other time that he happened to displease a majority of Council. This background helps to explain why the jobs of clerk and treasurer have frequently been made almost as permanent as that of a Magistrate or Judge in Canada.

Yet there is some substance to the suggestion that a permanent official who is too secure in his job may assume an arbitrary and dictatorial attitude toward his local Council. This he may even do unintentionally merely because he feels he knows more about his special field than inexperienced Councillors do. Yet times change and the fresh winds of democracy may sweep in a Council with ideas that are newer and more responsive to the people's needs than his are. Hence, being able to appoint and remove its own officials is one of the most important self-governing powers a local Council can have. It is clear, then, that if the modern need for trained personnel is to be met adequately, a delicate balance must be reached somewhere between annual appointment and absolutely permanent tenure. And Councils must be aware of the serious responsibility of making sound appointments on the basis of merit.

A Variety of Provisions

Provincial Legislatures in Canada do not seem to have settled upon a solution to this very difficult problem. At present the laws contain a wide variety of provisions for the appointment and removal of different types of local officers. In most provinces the law rides off in both directions at once. While certain officers, such as clerks and treasurers, have tenure during good behaviour, all others, as the law puts it, "hold office during pleasure, and may be dismissed at any time by resolution of the Council". In some of the smaller municipalities they must even be reappointed annually. The fact that certain specialists are hard to replace means that they are not likely to be dismissed lightly. But having full-time experts holding office "during pleasure" raises the question whether good men will be attracted to key positions without stronger protection against arbitrary action by a small majority on a Council.

Finding and Arranging Personnel

In addition to this problem of tenure, two others come crowding in upon local government as the number of civic employees grows. One is that of *finding* personnel who are expert enough to perform the complicated tasks modern local government requires. The other is that of *arranging* them so that they may do the work most efficiently.

More and more it is being realized that the two really go together. In other words, municipalities can't expect all their employees to be trained experts with great executive ability, and couldn't afford to pay them if they were. Hence, they must hire *one* expert in each field to head up the activity and put him in charge of all the employees concerned with that activity. A few of the more capable and experienced employees are placed beneath him, and they direct the others in a descending pyramid of control. This is really what is meant by an administrative "department". The cities, through sheer numbers of employees, have been forced to organize their personnel in this way already. The fewer the departments the simpler, more understandable and more workable the organization becomes.

A City or Town Manager?

Experts in public administration argue that even in the cities this process of business-like organization has not been carried to its logical conclusion. If it is more efficient to have only a few departments with an expert at the head of each, why would not their work be further simplified by having an able executive officer at the head of them all?

Most Councils in Canada control their departments by having a standing committee supervise each department head. This means that the committee must do two jobs at once—and may do neither properly. Not only may it be neglecting its real job—helping Council decide on policy—it may also, through meddling in details, short-circuit the department head's control over the execution of the policy. In addition, the Council as a whole may get only a broken jig-saw picture of how its decisions are being carried out. If all the department heads were required to deal with a single full-time executive officer and then *he* reported to Council, the latter would get a much clearer view of what is going on. Council's policies would be more unified and consistent, and departmental activities would be better co-ordinated. This, in brief, is the argument for the City or Town Manager.

In the United States the Council-Manager plan has been spreading rapidly since the war and is now used in about half of the cities. It has also been adopted by about half of the medium-sized cities in Canada. Of course, most of Canada's smaller municipalities already have what amounts to the Manager plan for, as we have seen, the clerk-treasurer plays the role of Manager. But the plan has made little headway in large cities.

Going to School

Municipalities in Canada, then, are beginning to realize the importance of concentrating responsibility for carrying out Council's business in a few top-flight officers instead of many mediocre ones. In several fields of municipal activity, however, there are simply no such persons available. This is really one of the biggest problems that local government in Canada is facing today. The only solution, obviously, is to give schooling in these specialized municipal professions.

Two methods may be used: schooling while in service (called *inhouse* training), and courses before appointment (sometimes called *outhouse* training!). A start has been made on both. Many of the provinces, often in co-operation with the universities, hold short in-service training courses each year for clerks and treasurers, assessors, health officers, etc. And some universities now offer post-graduate courses to would-be experts in these fields. For example, some universities have set up programmes to train badly-needed planning officers, and Queen's has an Institute of Local Government.

Attracting and Keeping Personnel

Related to the problem of making trained personnel available is that of attracting and keeping capable civic servants. Most employees desire security, and they will go where they can find it. Municipalities must therefore be prepared to offer conditions of work just as attractive as those in private employment. This ties in with the problem of tenure, for an able person who felt he would be at the mercy of a fickle Council would not be likely to offer his services to a municipality.

Another aspect of security is provision for old age. Until recent years municipalities made no systematic provision for pensions, and regarded a small pension as a special reward for long and faithful service, requiring special consideration and approval because of the cost. This procedure not only left municipal officers in an insecure position, but, more important, the added cost had the effect of encouraging Councils to maintain public servants long past the period of their useful employment.

For these reasons the provinces have passed laws enabling municipalities to set up contributory pension plans for their employees. Under such a plan both a municipality and its employees contribute into a fund which is used to pay pensions. Most of the large cities have managed to set up plans of this kind, but most other local units have not succeeded in doing so. One difficulty in starting a plan has been providing for those who are already past or close to retirement age. A more important problem is that the smaller municipalities can't afford such a plan. The solution, as for teachers, is a province-wide plan, with the employees, the municipalities, and the province sharing the cost—like the one begun by Ontario in 1963. Within three years 33,000 municipal employees had joined Ontario's plan—a good indication of the need for such a plan.

Employment Rules

Any municipality that has a large number of employees— Montreal alone has over 15,000—must also try to establish a fair and attractive system of employment rules dealing with such things as hours, leave and working conditions. Here one of the most difficult "nuts to crack" is that of setting up a fair system of promotion. There are many trade unions among Canada's civic employees and they have done much to improve wages and working conditions. They argue that hiring and promotion should not be left to an inexpert elected committee or even to the whim of a single department head. In promotion or rehiring, they say *seniority* (length of service) should be a deciding factor. Yet it is clear that to ensure a vigorous, efficient public service *ability* and *training* are equally important.

Some cities in the United States have tried to solve this problem, as well as that of hiring on the basis of merit, through the use of Civil Service Commissions like those at the provincial and federal levels of government. A few Canadian cities have also set up such a system — notably Montreal.

Salaries for Service

None of these measures for attracting and keeping able civic employees, however, touches the major problem of pay. In all but the larger cities, municipalities usually cannot meet the salaries offered for comparable work in private employment. A partial solution, as already suggested, might be to substitute someone expert at two or more jobs for several mediocre or part-time people. For example, medium-sized units could employ persons trained as both engineer and assessor. But many small municipalities could not even afford this solution.

THE PERSONNEL OF THE COURTS

Courts are Part of the Municipal System

Important among those who complete the job are the personnel of our law courts. It is they who, in an important sense, *really* finish the job. For it is they who finally straighten out the relationship between citizens and their municipalities. If a municipality takes a man's property in order to build a new street, for example, it is the Courts who finally decide how much it must pay him. Or if a man feels that a municipal assessor has over-valued his property for tax purposes, the Courts have the final say as to its proper value. And to penalize or protect local citizens who are accused of breaking by-laws, the Courts are indispensable. In this sense, the lower Courts are really part of the municipal system.

Judiciary Must be Impartial

The reason they are often not thought of as such is that in Canada the judiciary are all appointed by the senior governments (all County Court and higher Judges by the federal government and all others by the provinces), and almost all hold their jobs during good behaviour. They are not appointed or elected locally as is the custom in many parts of the United States. We in Canada are confident that ours is the better plan. It prevents local favouritism, since Justices have no fear of losing their jobs at the next election if they make decisions or give judgments that displease certain local people.

For persons important enough to have the final say on the right or wrong of actions between individuals, everything must be done to ensure that they will be able to see both sides of a question at once. They must be absolutely impartial. This is much more likely to be true if they are not financially or socially dependent upon particular groups or persons in the local community. Yet there are still a few minor court Justices in Canada who hold office during pleasure, work only part-time and collect fees rather than a salary for their work. This means that they must support themselves by having other jobs too—other business relationships in the community. The provinces concerned are rapidly remedying this situation by replacing these part-time Justices with full-time Provincial Judges or Magistrates.

A Difference of Degree

In order to do their work the Courts in most provinces are organized into three main levels: a Supreme Court of the Province, County Courts and such lower courts as Provincial Courts (called Magistrates' Courts in some provinces) and Small Claims Courts. In larger centres the Provincial Courts are frequently further divided into separate Provincial Criminal Courts (in some provinces still called Police Courts) and Family and Juvenile Courts.

The Provincial Courts deal with most criminal cases, and the main difference between them and the higher Courts lies in the seriousness of the offences with which they deal. In many cases, if you think a decision given in the lowest Court is unjust, you can appeal to the County Court, and sometimes from the County Court to the Supreme Court of the

Province. Some — for example murder cases — can be tried only by the Supreme Court, but preliminary hearings may be held in the lower Courts. Also, of those which may go directly to the Supreme Court, many can be tried in the County Court if the parties agree. Often a dispute can be settled more quickly and cheaply in the lower Court.

The Supreme Court of the Province usually holds only one or two sittings a year in a particular locality, while the County Courts sit about once a month and the lower Courts every week or two, or even daily in larger centres.

Magistrates and Sheriffs

Since the Supreme Courts usually decide matters of province-wide concern, our main interest is in the personnel of the lower Courts. Who are they and what do they do?

While a County Court is presided over by a Judge, a lower Court may still be presided over by two Justices of the Peace (who collect only fees) or by a Stipendiary Magistrate (paid a stipend, often by a municipality) or, more usually, by Magistrates or Provincial Court Judges (who are paid a salary by the province). In towns and cities the latter may also, besides trying cases, have a good deal to do with supervising the local police and with helping to hear assessment appeals. Sometimes the municipal solicitor or clerk still doubles as Magistrate or Deputy Magistrate.

The County or District Court House, which in some provinces is maintained jointly by the municipalities in the County or District, and in others is maintained directly by the province, houses the office of the Sheriff, who is the executive officer of the Court. His job is to do the less pleasant work of enforcing the law. If someone is to be summoned, the Sheriff must do it. If someone is ordered to pay a fine, the Sheriff collects it. If someone refuses to pay a fine, the Sheriff must, if the Court so orders, seize and sell his goods. And he must keep a careful record of all his legal actions. Furthermore, he must keep order in Her Majesty's Court, and look after the prisoners. If a prisoner escapes, he is to blame; if a prisoner has to be taken to jail, he or one of his constables must take him. He must also summon a jury when one is needed, from a list of citizens drawn up for the purpose. (Incidentally, when one reads the list of exceptions in some provincial laws — often including all women, clergymen, doctors, druggists, dentists, teachers, professors, pilots, marines and dozens more—one wonders how a jury list is ever made up at all.)

Such, then, are the many and varied tasks of the Sheriff. Yet he may be only a part-time official of the province, collecting one or two thousand dollars a year in fees. In most provinces, however, in return for turning all fees over to the province, he is paid a fixed salary. In towns and cities the chief of police, who is appointed and paid by Council, performs many of the duties that would ordinarily fall to the Sheriff.

Another Question

Municipalities do, of course, retain money collected in fines for the infraction of by-laws. But the amount is small compared with their costs. In most provinces, except for the salaries of Judges and Magistrates, municipalities must pay all or a large share of County and lower Court costs not covered by fees — including costs for the Court House, jail, clerk, criers, registrars, juries, Sheriff, solicitor, coroner, constables, inquests and prosecutions. Federal or provincial appointment of those who apply and interpret the law of the land is no doubt a good thing. It gives the judiciary independence. Whether at the same time the municipalities should be paying such a large part of the bill for the administration of justice is another question.

7. How They Get Their Money

A Price and a Tax

Municipal Councils must, of course, collect money to pay for the many activities in which they engage. The main difference between the way a business and a government collects money for the services it gives is that the one asks a price while the other demands a tax. A distinctive feature of the tax is that it is compulsory. Many of the services that Councils perform for the community either would not be supplied at all, or would be supplied inadequately, if buying them were allowed to be a matter of individual choice. As Samuel Johnson once explained, "A tax is a payment exacted by authority from part of the community for the benefit of the whole."

Yet there are many examples of payments made to governments which are more in the nature of a price than a tax. The payment of rates for electricity only by those who use the service is one. In fact, local governments in particular have a whole series of different kinds of charges whose degree of compulsion varies according to how much direct service is received in return. Some are purely voluntary payments for a specific service received (like the fee for admission to a civic golf course). Others are partly compulsory and partly related to benefit received (like the special levy on abutting property for paving a street at the request of a majority of the owners).

Sources of Revenue

The most common and the most important sources of revenue, however, are the compulsory taxes which have little or no relation to benefit received (like the tax on property for the support of schools, which even a bachelor must pay). This is well illustrated by the following figures, based on Statistics Canada estimates for 1972, showing municipal current revenues from various sources:

	$ Millions	Per Cent
1. Real Property Tax	3,335	36.5
2. Business Taxes	320	3.5
3. Special Assessments (owner's share)	273	3.0
4. Other Taxes (incl. poll, personal property, sales and amusement)	114	1.2
TOTAL TAXATION	4,042	44.2
5. Grants from Senior Governments	4,415	48.4
6. Sales and Services	359	3.9
7. Other (incl. licences, permits, fines, enterprises, etc.)	317	3.5
TOTAL REVENUES	9,133	100.0

Note that taxes account for only 44 per cent of total municipal revenues but that most of this comes from a single type of tax—the levy on real property.

In one important sense this gives an exaggerated idea of the part taxes play in municipal finance. The reason is that the revenues and expenditures of the many urban undertakings run partly independent of municipal Councils are not brought into the main municipal accounts. Thus, only the *net* revenues (or deficits) of water or electric power commissions are counted as municipal revenue, and only the *net* deficits of municipally owned hospitals and cemeteries are counted as municipal expenditure. The total revenues of such utilities and services, then, would add several hundred million dollars to the total monies that municipal authorities are responsible for collecting.

A growing source of municipal revenue is provincial subsidies, now larger than the total of local taxation. Although the provinces have long aided local governments through large special-purpose grants (paid mainly to school boards for education), it is only in recent years that the need for contributions to the general revenues of municipalities has been generally recognized. In 1972 these contributions totalled about $347 million, or 3.8 per cent of municipal revenue. But they are still insignificant compared with the special-purpose grants, which totalled more than ten times that amount, at $3.8 billion.

Comparing the revenues of the rural and urban units, one finds that the former depend almost exclusively upon the property taxes and provincial grants, while the latter find it possible to collect large sums in other ways. Of importance mainly to the urban units are income from: (1) business taxes; (2) licences, permits, fees, and franchises; and (3) fines and law enforcement. The greater revenue of the urban units from law enforcement is to be expected in view of their higher costs for police protection.

Although rural governments receive some income from these categories, they collect almost nothing from the two most lucrative sources of additional revenue in cities—amusement and sales taxes, and income from public utilities. The former are used mainly in Newfoundland, Quebec and Saskatchewan, while the latter is most significant in the towns and cities of Western Canada.

Since the income from utilities is *net* income (after payment of costs), apparently most urban utilities are being run at a profit. What this really means is that the users of the utilities, through higher rates, are contributing to the general expenditures of urban Councils. In other words, they are paying taxes indirectly and thereby easing the burden on the taxpayer. This may seem unfair to the users, but in practice the user group and the tax-paying group overlap to a large extent so that, if not carried too far, the main result is a less painful method of extracting taxes from the public.

A False Profit?

It is hard to know, however, whether these utilities really are making a profit. For one thing, many of them don't pay the municipalities a full share of property and business taxes. And because it is hard to decide precisely how much money should be set aside for replacing plant and equipment, Councils are tempted not to set aside enough, in order to collect a larger "profit". Hence they may in future be called upon to subsidize utilities which they falsely believe are making profits now.

The recent trend has been to set up commissions which operate their utilities more independently of Councils. However, it is doubtful whether such a development will clear up the situation. It may merely lead to an undesirable division of control. For it is usually the municipality's credit which puts such utilities on their feet and it is the municipality which must take the risk of loss. Hence, they don't really become independent. And elected Councillors convincingly argue that a proper serving of the public's interest in such a service requires that it be directly under their supervision and control. The best solution, then, appears to lie in the further development of modern accounting practices so that Councils will know exactly how the utilities stand financially.

Poll Tax Puzzle

Although the Maritimes are the only provinces in Canada where the poll tax is still used to any extent, because of its long history a word should be said about it. This tax is a flat annual payment of so many dollars levied mainly upon males over 21 and under 60 who don't pay property taxes. Often women are not included, even women who are employed. This discrimination in favour of the ladies is doubtless a hang-over from the days preceding their "emancipation". Although limits have been set by the provinces, the actual amount of the tax is usually decided by the local Council (and may range anywhere from $2 to $10).

The justification for this tax is that, since everyone benefits from municipal services, everyone who earns an income should be asked to contribute to their support. Yet in most cases it takes no account of whether a person is earning an income. It is also very difficult to collect, especially in urban areas, where people move about from place to place, or live in one place and work in another. For example, Sydney not long ago complained to the Nova Scotia Legislature that many of her workers claimed residence in the municipality of Cape Breton, in order to avoid the higher city poll tax. Moreover, even if poll-taxers (mainly lodgers) were not asked to pay, they would still be contributing indirectly to their municipality in other ways. They would contribute to landlords' taxes through room rents and board, and they would be paying federal and provincial taxes, a share of which is returned to the municipality in the form of grants and services.

Hence, perhaps the most convincing argument in favour of the tax is that, since it is a *direct* payment to municipalities, it gives its payers a greater interest in local government, and in particular a more responsible interest in careful municipal financing. This view would have more substance if the poll tax were made to vary with the tax rate. For then poll-taxers would be made more conscious of annual increases in expenditures.

THE TAX ON PROPERTY

The Real King-Pin

As we have seen, the real king-pin of municipal finance is the tax on real property. Compared with it, all other local sources of revenue pale into insignificance. It is therefore important for us to know more about this lucrative tax.

In the first place, it is one of the most ancient and venerable of government taxes. In the old days it was shared with senior governments, and was a *general* tax upon wealth of every description at a rate which varied according to how much money a government needed. Thus, if the wealth of a community was calculated to be $100 million and its government needed to raise $1 million, the tax rate would be $1 on each $100 worth of a man's property. This was thought to be fair because those who possessed more wealth than others paid more (in dollars — but not, as with modern income taxes, *in proportion* to their wealth). One can see what a tremendous source of tax revenue this could be.

As industries and corporations grew, however, the value of property became increasingly hard to measure. More and more wealth became transformed into intangible (paper) wealth — into stocks, bonds, mortgages, notes, bank accounts and what not. This meant it could not easily be found, valued, or attributed to the proper owner. Also, the owners of a company might be living in one place while their business was in another and it was hard to say to which municipality they should pay their taxes. These developments finally led the senior governments to invent new taxes for intangible forms of wealth and income, and to leave the property tax with the municipalities. In practice it became restricted to a tax only on *real* property (land, buildings and other improvements) and on real *personal* property (belongings, furnishings and equipment). This, then, is substantially the form in which the property tax is used in Canada today.

For Use and for Business

The tax on personal property, however, is an extremely hard one to apply fairly. For one thing personal property is hard to find, value properly and keep track of. No ordinary assessor, for example, could value precious jewellery or rare paintings. And the furnishings in a building often belong to tenants who must be recorded separately and who may move frequently. Besides, in urban areas the most valuable type of "personal" property is the stock, equipment and machinery of businesses and factories. What the tax does, then, is lump together two quite different kinds of "personal" property—that acquired for personal use, and that owned for business purposes. It applies the same (general property) tax rate to both. Yet there is good argument for applying a special kind of tax to businesses.

For these reasons, in all but the non-city units in Manitoba and Nova Scotia, the personal property tax had been abandoned in Canada and replaced by a business tax, and in some cases also a household or tenant tax. These taxes are levied upon the tenants rather than upon the owners of the property. And they are levied at the general rate upon a value which at first represented roughly the value of the business or household equipment, but now is usually calculated as a percentage of the value of the real property occupied. Halifax, for example, replaced the personal property tax with a business tax on 50 per cent of the assessed value of business property, and also for some years a household tax on 10 per cent of the assessed value of housing. Although this arrangement collected more from business than did the personal property tax, it did not recognize that the size and income of a business may have little relation to the value of the property it occupies.

Other cities and towns in Canada have therefore tried other ways of relating the value to the business. In some, as in Ontario, the percentage of value upon which the rate is levied varies according to the type of business. Others, as in Quebec and Manitoba, apply the rate to the annual rental value of the premises. Still others, as in Saskatchewan, measure the total floor space occupied. But almost all of them, it will be noted, relate the tax to the value or size of the property occupied rather than to the size or income of the business. In other words, the municipal business tax is still primarily a property tax and takes little account of "ability to pay".

Whether the *general* tax on real property should also make a distinction between residential and business property is an interesting question. Thus Halifax for some years applied a much lower rate to residential than to business property. The one was fixed at $3.50 per $100 of value while the other was nearly three times that, and rose according to the spending requirements of the city. The result was that, while the burden on housing was eased, the tax on business became too high, so the fixed rate on housing was abandoned. Elsewhere in Canada, usually the same rate is applied to both types of property.

The Hidden Subsidy

Many kinds of property are exempt from taxation, usually including properties of charitable, religious, educational, health and welfare bodies and of the federal and provincial governments. These exemptions become more and more valuable to their holders as the costs of local government, and hence tax rates, rise. What they mean in effect is that the rest of the local community, by supplying those exempted with free services, are indirectly paying them a hidden subsidy.

Exemption is a particularly difficult problem where the concentration of exempt property is unusually high. A few towns and cities, such as Ottawa and Halifax, contain such large tax-free educational, religious and especially government properties that the value of exempt property may even be greater than that which is taxable.

The argument for exemption is that the activities of tax-exempt bodies, besides deserving encouragement and support, often bring prestige, business and employment to a community. But this does little to ease the burden of cost on the local government and its taxpayers. Besides, it is questionable whether a local municipality should be expected to subsidize so heavily institutions which may serve a much wider area.

In recent years the federal government and most provinces have partially recognized these arguments with respect to government properties by making payments to the municipalities in lieu of taxes on these properties. But the federal government doesn't pay on all of its property and pays only where the value of its eligible property exceeds 4 per cent of the value of all taxable property. The provincial grants may be restricted to certain types of provincial property such as revenue-producing enterprises. Hence, municipalities justifiably complain that the payments still are not nearly large enough to make up for their tax losses on exempt property, and that their subsidies to the owners of such property should not be hidden in this way.

Partial Exemptions

Certain kinds of property may be taxed on only part of full value, in order to aid either the owners or the economic activities associated with the property. Thus in Nova Scotia the working tools of tradesmen and mechanics, and the property of widows, deserted wives and persons over 65, are taxed on only the value above a certain sum. In the four Western provinces, because of the early influence of the theory that only land should be taxed, buildings and other improvements are taxed on only a portion of their value. The portion ranges mainly from 60 per cent in Saskatchewan to 75 per cent in some British Columbia municipalities. And in the three prairie provinces, farm buildings are still entirely exempt. The consequent loss in revenue partly explains the greater dependence on income from public utilities in the West.

Another important type of partial exemption is the "fixed assessment". Until recent years it was the custom for urban Councils in Canada to make concessions to industries, or to desired enterprises like rinks or hotels, through agreements exempting a large percentage of their property from taxation for a specified number of years.

In the case of industries, the fixed assessment was granted in order to attract a new industry to a municipality, the theory being that infant industries need such financial encouragement while they are going through their "growing pains". But many industries in Canada seem to have had a rather long weaning period. The practical result of leaving municipalities free to make their own terms with new industries was unhealthy competitive bidding among local units in the form of higher or longer exemptions. It is questionable whether municipalities are financially strong enough to afford such subsidies, beyond the first few years at least. Most provinces therefore now either prohibit such exemptions or restrict them in new agreements, and some specify that fixed assessments must increase each year until they reach full value (after, say, ten years). But even where there is provincial regulation, Councils sometimes fix assessments through informal agreements that are not publicized.

How It Is Collected

So much for property that is *not* taxed. But what is the procedure for collecting taxes on the billions of dollars worth of property that *is* subject to taxation in Canada?

One of the most significant things about the whole taxing process is how elaborately it is laid down in the law. Most provinces have long Assessment Acts; and in these one can see that much has been done to ensure that the rights of property ownership are dealt with respectfully and that a man will not be forced to pay taxes wrongfully. The procedure is divided into three distinct steps: assessing, levying, and collecting. It is substantially the same in all provinces, but there are variations in detail. The exact procedure in any one province may therefore vary from that described here.

The First Step

Assessing is the process of recording and valuing property. Thus every year the assessor must make up a *roll* in which he records all the parcels of real property (land and buildings) in his district and his estimate of their value. Near the end of the year, after the assessor has completed his roll, he officially forwards it to the municipal clerk. He is also required to serve upon each person assessed a notice showing, among other things, the amount of the assessment.

In valuing any property, the assessor must, according to law, estimate its "actual" value. However, since it is difficult to make a really correct estimate, the untrained assessor is usually content with making sure his valuation is consistent with that for properties of *the same class*. In other words, he tries at least to ensure that like properties in a district have like assessments. This is one principle of fairness. But what is the effect on the owners of properties that are not alike—say, the valuable and the poor property? Or what about owners subject to the same tax rate but living in different assessment districts?

Despite provincial laws, most municipalities in Canada assess properties at just a fraction of their actual value.[1] If this fraction were the same for all properties and assessment districts, all ratepayers would be treated fairly, since the only difference from assessment at full value would be a higher tax *rate*. Each would still be paying the same total tax as at full value. If, however, small properties are assessed at three-quarters of the actual value and large ones at only half, then the real tax rate on the *full* value of the large ones is no longer as high as that on the small ones. This sort of thing very often happens when assessments are far below actual value. For then there is no standard by which to go *other* than that of like properties. Even if no unethical influences are in evidence, untrained assessors are likely to underestimate the value of wealthy properties because they fear that their estimates will be challenged in court, or simply because they are not used to dealing in large figures.

Similarly in the case of area-wide rates such as are levied by Counties, if the fraction varies from one unit to another, the ratepayers in each are paying a different real tax rate. For this reason a district or municipality is tempted to keep its assessments low, relative to others in the same area. But the others, realizing this, try to do the same. And a vicious circle of "competitive under-assessment" develops. The conscientious assessor who tried to keep his assessment nearer actual value would only be penalizing the ratepayers of his district — especially since the whole process leads to a lower and lower over-all valuation and hence to a higher and higher tax rate. The basing of large provincial grants on assessment and on the principle that where a district's assessment is low the need is greater and the grant should be higher, as with education grants, has worsened the situation; for districts are tempted to keep their assessments low to gain a larger grant.

---

[1] Historically, this occurred because assessors and Councils feared that a drop in property values would result in assessments *above* actual values and hence loud protests from the ratepayers. Since assessments are not revised upward annually, the recent inflationary rise in property values has worsened the situation.

Thus it can be seen that a good assessor must be a man of character, ability and training. He must be neither easily swayed nor afraid of having his estimate challenged by appeal. At the same time, valuation standards must be clearly defined and applied uniformly throughout a taxing area. In recent years, therefore, some provinces have been helping the municipalities to train assessors and have been urging them to adopt uniform valuation standards and to reassess properties. Other provinces, such as Prince Edward Island, New Brunswick, Ontario and the prairie provinces, have gone so far as to centralize the valuation of properties entirely in provincial hands, and Prince Edward Island even levies and collects the taxes for its municipalities.

The Right of Appeal

After the assessment notices have been sent out, a ratepayer has a fixed time within which he may appeal his assessment if he feels that it is too high or otherwise incorrect. Or this may be done by one of his neighbours — for an opposite reason, of course. Appeal is made, first, to a so-called Court of Revision, which often consists of the local Council or of members appointed annually by Council. If the ratepayer disagrees with the assessment as revised by one of these bodies, he may appeal to a higher authority, usually a County Court. In most provinces he may appeal a third time to an even higher Court, for a final decision.

Although this procedure is a valuable safeguard against injustice, to the average ratepayer it may become a cumbersome and costly business. Experts have suggested that if municipalities had well-trained chief assessors, much time and money could be saved by allowing them to hear informal appeals in the first instance. For then they would have a chance either to adjust mistakes quickly or to explain to the taxpayer why his assessment is what it is. This system, moreover, would make unnecessary the hearing of appeals by Councillors or annual appointees, who may be quite inexperienced at valuing property.

Others argue that not even the law courts are competent to question the value placed on a large property by a trained assessor. For this reason, in the prairies and in Ontario, only questions of law go to the Court of Appeal. Appeals on questions of fact with regard to value go to a special provincially appointed Assessment Commission or (in Ontario) Municipal Board.

"Striking the Rate"

When all appeals with respect to the assessment roll have been disposed of, the assessment is said to be "finally completed" as the basis for levying taxes. Obviously, this may take a very long time. Hence, last year's assessment roll must often be used as a basis for this year's tax levy.

Eventually, however, the time arrives for "striking the rate". In the spring of each year the treasurer submits to Council a statement of proposed expenditures for the year and of probable income from all sources other than the property tax. These estimates, called the budget, are reviewed by Council (usually first by its finance committee) and are revised, reduced or increased as Council sees fit.

Theoretically what Councils do first is determine the total amount of money required. Then the amount to be raised from the property tax is arrived at by deducting from this total the amount of other estimated revenues. In determining how much should be raised, Councils must, of course, make an allowance for taxes which may not be collectible. The tax rate is then arrived at by dividing the amount to be raised by the total of the taxable assessment.

If this easy problem in arithmetic were the only one Councils had to deal with in striking the rate, their lives would be simple. The real problem is how to keep the tax rate down and at the same time find enough money to pay for all the things that the community demands. The difficulty is twofold: to decide (1) whether the proposed expenditures should be cut, and (2) if so, what should be eliminated. The power of a Council to alter estimates *very much* in any year, however, is severely limited both by law and public opinion.

The Collector's Roll

After a tax rate has been "struck", the next step is for the clerk to calculate and enter the tax for each property upon a "collector's roll", which he has prepared from the assessment roll. All local improvement charges and all special and district rates are then added. When all the entries have been made he hands the roll to the tax collector (or collectors) as his authority for demanding payment. The collector must then send a tax notice to each person liable for taxes as shown on his roll. Often in small municipalities the clerk-treasurer is also the tax collector.

Since taxes are regarded as a necessary evil, the laws have had to be stern about tardy payment. Interest-rate penalties are always charged for arrears, and discounts up to 8 per cent may be allowed for prepayment or payment when due. But these provisions favour ratepayers with ready cash. Urban municipalities are therefore beginning to recognize, by providing for payment by instalment, that most of their taxpayers have monthly incomes. If taxpayers refuse to pay, after a certain period the collector may sue for taxes, or levy by court warrant and "distress" (seizure and sale of goods and chattels). In Nova Scotia, if there are no goods to seize, the ratepayer may even be put in jail.

Finally, by a specified date, the collector turns his roll over to the treasurer together with an account of all taxes still unpaid and the reasons why. Collection from then on rests with the treasurer, who after a fixed period may sell by public auction property seized for taxes. The proceeds of the sale are used to cover the tax arrears, penalities and costs of sale.

This procedure may sound rather harsh for the unfortunate ratepayer. However, the laws do provide several protective devices. Nova Scotia's Assessment Act, for example, states that "all beds, bedding, clothing, stoves, cooking utensils and the last cow" of any taxpayer in arrears are exempt from seizure. In some cases a Council may, for reasons of sickness, extreme poverty or gross error in the roll, relieve a ratepayer from payment for a year. And in all provinces a ratepayer may within a year or two buy back his property sold at public auction, at the sale price plus interest and costs.

THE BUSINESS OF BORROWING

We have now described how Councils collect their taxes. But we have not yet discussed one other important way in which they get their money—by borrowing.

Among the many things that Councils do—particularly urban ones—is a good deal of construction. This sort of work, and hence the spending for it (called *capital* expenditure), is variable. Councils may do a great deal one year and practically nothing the next. Especially in the case of a big project, taxing for the whole of it the same year it is built would be next to impossible. The ratepayers couldn't stand the strain, and the tax rate would see-saw erratically from year to year. Besides, the thing that is built—whether it be a street or a filtration plant or a Court House—is not all used up in one year. Hence, it is logical to pay for it over a period of time. What Councils do, then, is borrow money for this purpose. They then pay off the loan plus interest at a later date.

The most common method of doing this is by selling bonds on which they must pay yearly interest, but which they need not buy back until long afterwards—say, thirty years. In order to have enough money on hand at that time, every year they must tax for and lay away a certain amount in a "sinking fund".

Financial Finagling

But there are a number of objections to this method of financing capital expenditures. One is that if over the years there are several series of bond issues for many different projects, the whole financial picture becomes blurred. Confused Councillors may not be sure which bonds fall due when or how much money should be saved to pay them. And the accumulation of money in the sinking fund may give them a false feeling of financial security. Rather than increase taxes to keep up the fund, they may be tempted to sell new bonds to pay off old ones. As a result, years after a public building has been replaced taxpayers may find themselves still paying for the old one.

The danger of a temporarily imprudent Council committing the ratepayers to years of increased taxes to pay for some unsound project has always been clearly recognized. Often municipalities must have the consent of both the ratepayers and a provincial authority before borrowing for capital expenditures. But even this does not ensure the proper handling of sinking funds. Although the provinces have restricted the ways in which these funds may be invested, difficulties still arise over how and where to invest them.

In recent years, therefore, the provinces have been urging municipalities to sell *serial* bonds. By this means a Council not only pays interest yearly but also redeems a certain number of bonds each year. The bonds are so arranged that the annual payments are about equal in size, and the last ones are paid off at the end of the life of the structure or project for which the money was borrowed. This means that projects are paid for while they are being used, and sinking funds are unnecessary.

A few municipalities in Canada have even gone so far as to try a "pay-as-you-go" policy for all improvements. They point out that in the long run large savings can be made in this way. A public improvement whose cost is $100,000 may actually cost the taxpayers two or three times that much if they must pay interest on bonds for 40 or 50 years. Pay-as-you-go, however, not only runs into the difficulty of fluctuating tax rates but also raises the issue whether the present generation should be asked to pay for permanent improvements.

A more workable solution, then, is to adjust the tax rate so as to pay cash for all recurring improvements, such as surfacing streets, and to finance long-term improvements on the "pay-as-you-benefit" principle, by means of serial bonds. This avoids the difficulties of complete pay-as-you-go, yet does prevent short-sighted Councillors from keeping present tax rates down at the expense of higher rates in future.

The Importance of Timing

One aspect of municipal borrowing is its power to create employment. By borrowing unused money during a slump and putting it to work on municipal projects, a Council at the same time puts unemployed men to work. Economists used to agree that the teeter-totter of prosperity and depression, characteristic of our modern economic system, would continue unless all levels of government co-operated to prevent it. What farseeing Councils should do during boom years, they said, is postpone all non-essential projects and keep debt down to make borrowing easier during a slump.

During the long post-war inflation period this, admittedly, was hard to do. Interest rates were low and municipal credit was good. At the same time municipal Councils, boards and commissions had a large backlog of construction projects inherited from the depression and the war with which the public insisted that they proceed. And several provinces provided large funds from which local authorities could borrow at low interest rates for certain types of project.

Although municipal debt declined steadily during the war, Bank of Canada estimates show a post-war jump in net debt from $860 million in 1946 to $2,100 million in 1954 (an increase of almost 150 per cent). This may indicate that municipalities took an over-enthusiastic plunge into building activity, forgetting that this was a period of full employment, high prices and scarce materials. Such a policy not only may have contributed to inflation by bidding these materials away from an already over-expanded private market; it has also left Councils with less to build in future years when their constructive action may be needed most — to take up a slack in private building activity.

However, the present threat of "stagflation" — economic stagnation and unemployment combined with inflation — mystifies not only local Councils but even the economists. It is difficult to say whether Councils should now hold back on capital projects so as not to contribute to inflation, or plunge ahead with them in order to maintain employment.

8. The Problem of Centralization

Today we are living in a fast-changing world in which the relations of each individual with the rest of mankind are rapidly growing into a complex web. Tangle each of these webs together and the result is our modern complicated society. In this world of closely associated communities-within-communities it is becoming more and more difficult to say which level of government—local, provincial or national—should do what for us, or how the financial responsibilities should be split.

The ever-widening interdependence of social and economic life means that, in order to cope with it, the three levels of government can no longer afford to remain independent of one another. They have had to co-operate in developing closely co-ordinated activities. In other words, in order to deal with the intricate network of social and economic life, they have had to knit much more closely together their strands of regulation and service. They, too, have become more interdependent. At the provincial-municipal level, since the provinces are legally superior to the local units, this growth of a closer relationship has been accompanied by a process that, rightly or wrongly, has been called *centralization*.

Its Forms

This centralization has appeared in two principal forms: increased provincial supervision of municipal activities, and provincial administering or financing of traditionally municipal services.

Evidence of the increase in provincial supervision has been the creation and expansion of provincial Departments of Municipal Affairs. Although created in the Western provinces during the early years of the century, it was not until the economic depression of the 1930's that such Departments really came into their own. By this time they had become established in one form or another in most of the provinces, and during this period their powers were further expanded.

Financial Watchdogs

Partly because of the financial difficulties that overwhelmed the local units during the depression, Departments of Municipal Affairs were at first mainly concerned with municipal finances and accounting. The provinces have always, of course, found it necessary to retain a good deal of control over municipal borrowing. But before the creation of the provincial Departments, large municipal loans had to be approved by special Acts of the provincial Legislatures. Applications for borrowing had therefore to be considered by a standing committee of the Legislature, and much of each Session's time was taken up in dealing with them. The committees complained that they did not have time to study in detail the financial positions of the municipalities concerned. Further, they found it impossible to deal with the applications according to any uniform general principle, especially since they were subjected to local pressures and were tempted to play favourites. Local officials, moreover, were forced to spend much time at the Legislature in connection with applications.

One of the most important reasons for creating the new Departments, then, was to allow the local units to borrow for specified purposes without having to apply to the Legislature. Borrowing now ordinarily required only the approval of the Minister of Municipal Affairs, who was advised by the full-time, permanent experts in his Department. This meant that the Legislature was relieved of an undesirably detailed control over the local units. The new arrangement was less cumbersome for the municipalities and at the same time enabled the provinces to retain a desirable regulation of borrowing. This type of supervision, by reassuring the investing public, improved the borrowing credit of the local units.

Another difficulty under which the local units laboured when dealing with the provinces and with one another was a lack of comparable information. Book-keeping often was done badly and for no good reason varied from place to place. A common feature of the Acts creating the Departments of Municipal Affairs, then, was to prescribe uniform methods of accounting and uniform annual returns to the provinces. This made it possible for the Departments to compile comprehensive annual reports of municipal statistics.

Through a series of conferences between provincial and federal experts begun in 1942, this advance has been carried further. A uniform municipal accounting procedure was worked out and adopted for the whole of Canada, and was then gradually introduced under the supervision of the provincial Departments. Without these improvements, necessary comparisons for making intelligent decisions on many financial problems would be next to impossible.

The Growth of Supervision

Besides finances and accounting, several other types of municipal activity have come under provincial supervision. Indeed, in some provinces the job of supervision has become so big that it has been divided between the Department of Municipal Affairs and a specially created body such as the Ontario Municipal Board or the Quebec Municipal Commission. And in some cases provincial authorities exercise very wide supervisory powers. The extreme example is Newfoundland, where the Minister or the Cabinet must approve, besides the borrowing of money, municipal by-laws and budgets, and may even require revised budgets. In Nova Scotia every municipal by-law must be approved by the Minister of Municipal Affairs, and in Quebec the provincial Cabinet may disallow any by-law. In Ontario, health by-laws must be approved by the Minister of Public Health, traffic by-laws by the Department of Highways, and zoning by-laws by the Ontario Municipal Board.

In addition to controls such as these over the by-law powers of Councils, the provinces have also gradually introduced controls over Councils' administrative staffs. The extreme case again is Newfoundland where the Minister has the right to approve the appointment and salary of key officials. But even in other provinces there are examples of provincial approval of certain appointments or of qualifications for appointment, and provincially established standards of qualification. In some cases certain officials can't be fired except with provincial approval, and in others provincial authorities may, under certain conditions, dismiss municipal officials, appoint others in their place and fix their rates of pay. Some provinces also limit the right of Councils to reduce the salaries of certain officers, and some give the final decision on rates of pay to the Courts or special boards of arbitration. In most cases, officials of the lower Courts, though they may be paid by the municipalities, are appointed and directed by the province.

These examples of provincial supervision, while not necessarily adding up to a high degree of provincial control of municipal activity across Canada, are impressive. Many of the financial controls were introduced at a time when drastic measures were required to prevent some of the municipalities from going into default and thus ruining the credit of all municipalities. It is now being recognized that the financial difficulties of the local units during the depression were pretty much unavoidable, simply because the taxpayers had empty pockets. And it may be that the time has arrived when some of these controls can be done away with. It is also being realized that the provinces can, through their supervisory agencies, in many ways lead, advise, educate and encourage the local units without directly controlling them. If provincial Departments of Municipal Affairs were staffed with experts sufficiently competent to impress local authorities, the latter would be only too pleased to seek and follow their advice. There would then be less need for regulation and control.

The Second Form

The second form of centralization — increased provincial administering and financing of municipal services — has gone on apace during this century. Some services have been taken over entirely in all provinces. Liquor control and highways are examples. In Nova Scotia, all bridges and roads, except urban streets, are built and maintained by the provincial government. Elsewhere the provinces have taken over the highways and make generous grants toward the building and maintenance of secondary roads and bridges. Other functions that are in the process of being taken over are assessment and the administration of justice.

The greatest change in higher-level participation, however, has occurred precisely in the three fields where municipalities spend most of their money — education, health, and welfare. These subjects have become so important in recent years that all levels of government — municipal, provincial, and federal — have been pushed into new activities connected with them. Indeed, the inter-level relationships have now become so complicated that, in order to show the nature of the increased participation by senior governments, the division of responsibility must be described for each field in turn.

The Division in Education

Under the federal division of powers in Canada's Constitution, the provinces have the right to control education. And they have always jealously guarded this right. It is true that the federal government shares with the provinces half the cost of post-secondary education, and gives them grants to extend the teaching of our two official languages. But otherwise it does very little in this sphere.

Between the provinces and the municipalities, on the other hand, one finds a completely dual division of responsibility. In the past, the objective of the provincial governments appears to have been to exert a maximum of control over public education while contributing a minimum to its support. Thus local educational authorities have been regarded as essentially agents of the province and their responsibility has been limited primarily to costly matters of school administration — the erection and maintenance of buildings and the appointment and payment of teachers. The provincial Departments of Education, on the other hand, prescribe curricula, and train, examine, grade and issue certificates of qualification to teachers. They are responsible for implementing the school Acts, and they supervise the local school bodies through the use of inspectors. Although some city School Boards appoint and pay inspectors, in all cases they are regarded as officers of the provincial Departments and must report annually or oftener.

Before the war, often the only financial assistance the provinces gave to local boards was in the form of incentive grants for various types of specialized training which provincial authorities from time to time had thought it desirable to encourage. For example, grants would be made to assist in the hiring of highly qualified teachers (often specialists in high schools). The result, however, was to "fertilize the tree at the top", as one educationist put it. Since the grants favoured the areas with the best facilities, they did little good for the rural districts and poorer schools, which needed help the most. The size of most school districts was so small, and their tax resources so limited, that they could not even provide adequate buildings or teachers' salaries, let alone specialists.

Almost a Revolution

Since the war, however, there has been almost a revolution in the administration and financing of education. In most provinces rural school districts have been greatly enlarged. And the provinces have increased their aid to local authorities to an extent greater than in the whole previous period since the establishment of free schools. Indeed, in 1972 the government of Prince Edward Island went so far as to replace the some two hundred local School Boards with only five Regional Boards, and took over the total cost of education. Elsewhere, although the proportion of aid varies greatly, on the average the provinces now pay about 50 per cent of the cost of local schools. Because of the inability of local boards to handle many wider-than-local problems, the provinces have also developed extensive educational activities of their own. These include adult education, the training of the blind and deaf, the provision of travelling school libraries, and the production and distribution of educational TV programmes, videotapes and films. As a result, the provinces now pay well over half the cost of elementary and secondary education in Canada.

The rapid rise in financial aid to local school authorities has meant the growth of a complex system of grants for various special purposes combined with general grants which are designed to raise facilities to a desirable minimum level across a province. The special-purpose grants, which came first, were intended to foster certain types of school or course or teacher. General grants may be made on the basis of pupil attendance, number of classrooms, or number of days taught per teacher or per class, with different rates for different types of school; or, as in Ontario, partly on the basis of assessment, with grants highest in a district where assessment is lowest. In addition, most provinces make grants or loans to School Boards to assist in the construction of schools. But whatever the result of the various bases for making grants, the approach to a province-wide minimum of educational opportunity is only approximate. And the increase in financial aid has necessarily resulted in increased regulation and supervision by the provinces over how the money is spent.

Since educational facilities have been traditionally provided by the local units, an important question is this: just how far can the provinces go in sharing the cost and administration of education without destroying local autonomy and initiative? The answer partly depends on whether the system of grants can be simplified in such a way as to reduce the number of strings attached. It also depends on whether local interest in education can be maintained. Here the Departments of Education have been wise in encouraging the formation of local Home and School Associations throughout the country. Their rise and rapid growth in recent years is a very hopeful sign.

The Division in Health and Welfare

The division of provincial-municipal responsibility in the fields of health and welfare has become particularly complex. This is true for two reasons: many health and welfare activities are new and, second, the federal government has also entered the field. In the old days governments were not expected to take much interest in health and welfare. And what services did exist were largely local. Now, however, we find a confusing array of services at all levels of government and much joint sharing of costs.

What part does government play today, then, in looking after persons who fall ill? Until recent years the state considered itself mainly responsible for those who are down and out. If the doctor sent you to a hospital and you or your relatives couldn't pay for treatment, your municipality would reimburse the hospital. Although many hospitals are privately owned, most cities have municipally-owned hospitals, and in the Western provinces many hospitals are owned and operated jointly by municipalities, through the regional governments in British Columbia, and elsewhere in special Hospital Districts.

In recent years the federal and provincial governments have contributed large sums to the building of local hospitals, and most provinces, in addition, own and operate special hospitals for mental and tuberculosis cases. Some, such as New Brunswick, Newfoundland and Nova Scotia also own and operate general hospitals. Newfoundland has a general hospital in St. John's and many scattered "cottage" hospitals. Nova Scotia has owned and operated the Victoria General in Halifax for many years, and now runs two other general hospitals.

Recognizing that unexpected hospital or medical costs are a blow to anyone, all of the provinces, with federal help, have introduced either compulsory hospital insurance or free hospital service plans, and several have also adopted either medical insurance or free medical service schemes. Through these, employees and their employers and the province pay premiums or taxes into a provincial fund, and then if people go to a hospital or a doctor, the fund pays the cost. Alberta's scheme was at first organized on a municipal basis. And for several years before the introduction of a province-wide plan, Saskatchewan had a number of municipal doctor schemes where the local doctor was hired on salary. It is interesting that these early schemes were created on a local basis.

Preventive Work

Looking after ill people, however, is a relatively new job for government. Until recently its main work in the field of health was the prevention of illness. For this purpose the basic organization at the local level is usually a system of Health Boards, one in each municipality. Through their power to pass regulations under the various health Acts, they can remove any conditions likely to lead to ill-health: stop people from throwing rubbish about, see that foodstuffs for sale are kept clean, that dead animals are buried, and so on. They also appoint Medical Officers and Sanitary Inspectors.

The job of the Medical Health Officer is to report on all cases of infectious diseases (which are first supposed to be reported to him), to quarantine homes, to close the school if he sees fit, to see that buildings are kept sanitary, indeed to do everything he can to prevent the spread of disease. On him probably more than on anything else depends the effectiveness of the local Boards. But in small units, his job is often only part-time and he is paid only a few hundred dollars a year; most of his time is taken up with private practice and he is not specifically trained for public health work.

Moreover, despite modern developments in public health, many of the local Boards have remained largely inactive. Here is the annual report of a rural Board, not so very many years ago:

"Gentlemen, I beg leave to submit the following report of the Board of Health for District No. 5: The general health of the District during the past year has been very good, with the exception of several cases of common colds.

Respectfully submitted,
John Doe
Chairman"

The result of this inactivity has been that the provincial governments have had to develop their own public health services. And some, such as those in Quebec and Nova Scotia, have divided their provinces into large regional Health Divisions and have appointed one or more trained Public Health Officers, aided by a staff of public health nurses, to each region. The staff and the work of the Departments of Public Health in the provinces have therefore grown by leaps and bounds. While the work that they do is, of course, necessary and desirable, unless some arrangement is worked out for sharing their activities with local government, it is likely that they will almost completely absorb the responsibility for public health.

The other provinces, in trying to avoid this development, have been creating enlarged municipal Public Health Units and then giving them substantial grants. In Ontario the Units are based on the County or metro area and elsewhere are of like size. They are administered by boards whose members are appointed by the County, metro or local municipalities. In one or two cases, however, there are provincially appointed members, and in most cases the Units' Health Officers and nurses are provincial civil servants.

For its part, the federal government for many years had made small grants-in-aid to the provinces for specific public health activities. In 1948 it established a new $30-million-a-year programme of federal grants, generally on a per capita basis (for health surveys, cancer, tuberculosis, and venereal disease control, treatment of crippled children, research, mental health care and hospital construction). Since then it has greatly increased these grants, has added new ones, and has taken on half the cost of health insurance. Also, its Department of Health and Welfare has developed many of its own preventive and health-building services, such as its food and drug research and national fitness programmes.

The Welfare Problem

It is perhaps in the field of public welfare, however, that the trend toward a three-way division of responsibility is illustrated most clearly. As early as 1927 the federal government began a joint Dominion-provincial scheme of old-age pensions, which were administered by the provinces but paid for on a shared basis. In some provinces, like Alberta and Manitoba, the provincial share was also partly paid by the municipalities.

Since 1941 the federal government has introduced welfare schemes financed and run entirely by itself. The major examples are unemployment insurance, the national employment service, family allowances, and old-age pensions for everyone at the age of 70. An indication of how important these are financially is the fact that the amount paid out in family allowances alone is almost as great as that spent on schools in the whole of Canada. And the Department of Health and Welfare, besides running some of these and other welfare programmes, does research on various aspects of welfare, including social security plans and guaranteed incomes.

The provinces, too, have well-developed welfare services. They administer old-age assistance for those between the ages of 65 and 70 and share with the federal government half (or more) of the cost. They pay mothers' allowances and provide for workmen's compensation in case of accident. Along with the municipalities, they make grants to private welfare institutions, and to local Children's Aid Societies for the care of neglected children. They are also basically responsible for correction services.

With all these schemes at higher levels of government supporting such a tremendous share of the welfare burden, one might think that in recent years municipalities have had little to do in the field of welfare. This, however, is by no means true. Some kinds of welfare are not provided for at all by higher-level schemes. As the senior governments saw the need for a net of social security services, they did what they could by stringing one rope at a time. But the net is far from complete. The recent investigations of poverty and proposals for guaranteed incomes show this. Even if the net were complete, many people in need of help would still fall through — would be unable to qualify for aid under one scheme or another. Hence, local authorities would still be responsible for looking after a large remainder of unfortunates.

Age on Their Side

One thing to be said for the existing welfare services at the municipal level is that they have age on their side. For some years after the Second World War, New Brunswick and Nova Scotia had a system of compulsory provision for the poor in rural parishes or districts that dated back to the first Poor Law in England, passed in good Queen Bess's time over

300 years ago. It's true, of course, that this system had improved considerably since Sam Slick's day in the 19th century. You may have read in Judge Haliburton's *The Clockmaker* how horrified Sam was at the "selling of the poor" in Nova Scotia. This was done by offering the poor at auction to the *lowest* bidder, that is, to the person who would take the least sum from public funds for keeping a pauper in his home. Sam Slick claimed that it was worse than negro slavery in the U.S.A. But symbolic of how slowly the Maritimes moved away from this tradition is the fact that, until 1954, Nova Scotia's Poor Law contained a clause which insisted that "the Overseers shall not provide for the maintenance of the poor by putting up the same at public auction".

Under this former system, three "Overseers of the Poor" in each district decided who was to get aid and to what extent. And proving that you deserved aid was a rather grim business. First of all, you had to show that you were really down and out. If you had any property the Overseers could take it to help to pay for your keep. If they decided to house you in the County Home, your relatives, down to your grandchildren, were supposed to pay as much as possible toward your board. Second, you had to show that you belonged to the district that was required to support you. This meant, usually, that you had to show that you had paid taxes there or had lived there for a number of years. If you couldn't prove this you were out of luck and had to apply to the Overseers in the district to which you did belong, if any. This involved a lot of trouble and humiliation for many decent people.

While the provisions for local relief were not as antiquated as this in most of the other provinces, nevertheless they had not been improved very much by the end of the war. For example, although the best welfare practice favoured keeping the needy in their own homes, often the form of local relief in Canada was maintenance in a municipal or County Home, or payment toward maintenance in a private institution. Many of these Homes and institutions were not designed to segregate different kinds of needy persons. Indeed, in the Maritimes many County Homes were combined poor homes and asylums. In some cases a single building housed invalids, aged and "harmless insane" persons, crippled and mentally defective children, and normal orphans.

In general, then, although some of the large cities have very modern and well-developed welfare departments, local governments in Canada have found it difficult to develop their services in keeping with modern welfare standards. Since the war, however, the provinces have been helping the local units with greatly increased financial aid. In British Columbia, for instance, this aid amounts to 80 per cent of the local cost, and, as a condition of receiving aid, all municipalities above a population of 10,000 must have their own social welfare departments. The provinces have also greatly expanded their own welfare services, and some have decentralized their Departments of Welfare into regional divisions, with a staff of social workers for each region.

An Over-all Approach

Despite the inability of most local units to provide adequate public health and welfare services, there are good grounds for the belief that as much health and welfare work as possible should be performed by local authorities. For it is in these fields that government touches the lives of citizens most intimately. Schemes administered by separate authorities may mean that a citizen who is ill or in need has to deal with several agencies just when his case may require an over-all approach, a total understanding of his local situation. Moreover, if the higher levels of government continue to develop their own services, and to by-pass the municipalities, the strength of local government will suffer.

Too often in these fields local authorities are regarded merely as bill-paying agencies. Until recent years, for example, municipalities were required to pay part of the cost for indigents in provincial health and welfare institutions. This requirement caused much red tape in verifying the residence of indigents, etc., and certainly needed to be dispensed with. Similarly, provinces that have not already done so could relieve the municipalities of all or most of their share of the cost for indigents in private health and welfare institutions, and for neglected children, without much loss of local autonomy. Municipal payment for a service adds nothing to the strength of local government if municipalities are given no control over how the service is provided.

Its Cause and Nature

In recent years it has been popular for local politicians and others to worry aloud about the dangers of centralization and the need for keeping autonomy. The facts already presented show that there is no doubt a good deal in what they say. But words like "centralization" and "autonomy" carry emotional tones and are difficult to define. They are examples of what have been aptly called "weasel" words—words so slippery that, as Alice's Humpty Dumpty said, they can mean whatever you want them to. Just as all aspects of local autonomy are not necessarily good, all aspects of centralization are not necessarily bad. It is therefore important for us to examine the cause and nature of modern centralization so that, when considering examples of increased aid or activity by higher levels of government, we will know to what extent they may be regarded as undesirable.

Industrialization Is the Word

What, then, has been the cause of centralization? The answer, if given in a word, would probably be *industrialization*. Since the municipalities were first created the social and economic pattern of the whole country has become closely knit as a result of the growth of large-scale business and industry in the modern world. This growth has included the advent of motor-cars, modern communications, and the crowding of people into cities and towns. From our viewpoint, what, more particularly, have been the effects of this revolutionary development?

First have been the effects of the *physical* changes—the greater ease with which people travel and communicate. This has meant a greater feeling of provincial and national unity. Many services, such as education and highways, which were once mainly of local concern, now have a nation-wide aspect. And the feeling has grown that there should be a provincial if not a national minimum of social welfare. On top of this, improved travel and communication have made administration by the higher levels of government quite possible, while their specialization of knowledge, personnel and equipment has, for many services, made it seem desirable.

Second, and perhaps more important, have been the *economic* changes. These have increased the differences in wealth between individuals and between communities, and have shifted the preponderance of wealth in the country from one area to another. This has meant that many small, poor municipalities and school districts have been unable to bear the costs of the tremendously increased services that are expected of government. On the one hand, we all say that everyone should have a doctor's care when he's sick and a free bed in hospital if he can't pay, or that every child deserves a fair chance in school. On the other hand, the local taxpayers in these units just can't afford to pay for services at a desirable level—especially since the need for services is usually greatest in the poorest areas.

The problem can be partly solved by enlarging the local taxing unit to include areas with valuable property and then applying a uniform tax rate to the whole area. The burden will then fall less heavily on the taxpayers of the poor sections, for their services can be improved with money from the central pool. This explains why in many provinces the taxing unit for schools has been extended. Although this kind of extension is all to the good, one still finds significant differences in local tax resources among the extended units. Uniformly high standards of service therefore can't be achieved unless provincial grants to local units take account of these differences in revenue-raising ability.

Another economic change has been that the number of workers dependent upon insecure wage jobs has grown, and with it has grown the need for social security schemes and for social services of all kinds. At the same time, the rising standard of living means that citizens can now better afford such services. The local units, however, generally have failed to increase their social services in keeping with modern standards and with public demand. This, then, explains why the higher levels of government have had to step in with aid to education and have had to develop programmes for health and welfare.

Lucrative Taxes

But how is it that the higher levels have been in a position to extend their aid? This has resulted from another effect of industrialization. The forms of wealth have shifted from real land and improvements to intangible wealth and income. New forms of taxation have had to be developed: personal income, corporation, gasoline, motor vehicle, liquor and sales taxes, and succession duties. These can be much more easily and equitably collected by the higher levels of government. The accompanying shift in emphasis upon taxation according to ability to pay rather than benefits received, the unprecedented prosperity throughout the war and early post-war years, and the recent inflationary rise in prices, have all added tremendously to the lucrativeness of these forms of taxation.

The failure of local Councils to raise the level of their educational and social services resulted not only from their failure to see the need for better services, but also from local dependence upon a type of tax whose revenue-raising ability could not keep pace with the demand. The freedom of a local unit to decide in favour of better services depended upon its taxpayers' ability to bear taxes for supplying them. The freedom to decide was therefore in many cases only theoretical. Yet, aside from administrative difficulties, there is an obvious reason why the newer taxes should not be collected by local governments: if they were, some municipalities would be enormously rich, while others would be complete paupers. Also, an important reason for taxing at a higher level is to redistribute wealth from the rich to the poor units.

Sky-rocketing Revenues

The importance of the wartime shift of taxation revenue in favour of the senior governments can hardly be overestimated. Bank of Canada figures show that in the short period from 1930 to 1945, while municipal revenue increased by less than 18 per cent, provincial revenue jumped by over 140 per cent. Meanwhile, federal revenue had sky-rocketed to almost eight times its 1930 figure. Much of this tremendous expansion at the national level was, of course, made necessary by unprecedented wartime expenditures. Nevertheless, the wartime change in the relative position of the three levels was maintained during the early post-war period. For instance, in 1954 the federal share of total revenues was 66 per cent, the provincial share was 20 per cent, and the municipal, only 14 per cent.[1] The municipal share in 1930, on the other hand, had been almost 40 per cent. Since 1954 the federal share has declined as provincial revenues have expanded. But municipal revenues have never recovered their pre-war relative position. Indeed, they have not even kept pace with the general rise in prices. This means that the *real* amount of social and other services supplied by the municipalities from their own resources is actually less now than it was before the war.

The fact that municipal revenues have declined relative to those of the higher levels of government, however, does not necessarily imply that

[1] To avoid double counting in the total, general-purpose grants from a higher to a lower level of government (including the tax transfer payments) have been subtracted from the revenues of the higher level. Special-purpose grants to a lower level are *not* counted as revenue for that level.

municipalities today are in a financially weak position. The rising cost of services has been offset to a large extent by increased provincial aid and also by an impressive reduction in debt charges since the depression. Moreover, municipal revenues have been bolstered by the booming war and post-war economy; the increase in property values and incomes has, in some years, enabled local collections, including arrears, to leap to over 100 per cent of the current levy in many municipalities.

Yet it should be noted that throughout the war years the normal expansion of municipal services was prevented by shortages of labour and materials. Even maintenance activity was curtailed. This accounts for the wartime reduction in debt and relatively slow rise in expenditures. The increase in municipal activity since the war, combined with the rapid rise in costs, has meant that municipal surpluses have disappeared. Meanwhile, despite their rapid extension of social and other services, the senior governments have easily balanced their budgets, and some have enjoyed fat surpluses.

We are now in a position to sum up the results of the twentieth century social and economic changes as they apply to the problem of provincial-municipal relations. The facts are: (1) there is a strong demand for better local services, especially with respect to roads, education, health and welfare; (2) more and more of these services are coming to have a wider-than-local aspect; (3) central administration is now quite possible and, through the benefits of specialization, often appears to be relatively more efficient; (4) municipalities are in a reasonably strong, but not expanding, financial position; and (5) increasing emphasis upon revenues requiring wider-than-local collection has placed the senior governments in a financial position superior to that of the municipalities.

Since the war, increased general and specific grants from the federal government, plus their own expanding revenues, have placed the provinces in the position of being able to raise substantially the standards of necessary services. Many of these services, however, have been traditionally supplied by local governments. What, then, should the provincial-municipal arrangements be? How can the provinces raise the standards of provincial-municipal services without at the same time weakening local participation and control? In other words, can democracy be kept at home? This is the problem that has been created by centralization. In our final chapter we consider how this vital and pressing problem may be solved.

9. Can Democracy Be Kept at Home?

Guiding Principles

In trying to decide which level of government should perform a given service, there is little doubt that one of the guiding principles should be *efficiency* of performance. In the technical sense of efficiency, it is clear that today, because of modern specialization of equipment, knowledge and personnel, many existing municipal services would be performed more efficiently at a higher level. On the other hand, citizen-participation in government can be greater and the performance of services more responsive to citizens' needs when services are provided by local government. In other words, in the broader sense of efficiency—in the sense of *effectiveness* — local administration may be preferable.

Because of this conflict in our modern democratic society between the need for more technically efficient service and the need for greater responsiveness to local needs, no hard and fast rule can be drawn. The most desirable level for performance will to a large extent vary with the service. As Einstein would say, it's all relative. And in trying to decide whether a particular service should be local or provincial, the question to ask is: if it is made provincial, will the citizens lose more in one way than they would gain in another? For instance, the provinces' assumption of responsibility for building roads might make possible a highly efficient co-ordination of all arteries of traffic. But it is not likely that the efficiency gained by having urban streets built by the provinces would be enough to compensate for the loss of local control.

At the same time, while the degree to which services would be more efficiently performed by the provinces varies from service to service, the broader concepts of citizen-participation and responsiveness to needs affect *all* services. From this point of view, the more services that are locally controlled, the better. Hence, if there is doubt as to which level can perform a service most efficiently, preference should be given to local government.

There are, of course, various ways in which provincially administered services may be made responsive to local needs and wishes. One way of maintaining local contact is to have the details of action, although decided at the centre, carried out at the "grass roots". Thus a provincial department would maintain administrative offices in each community or region. This has been done in the case of several provincial services. And if technical efficiency is one of the chief objectives, it is a very desirable method of operation. Another method, which places less stress on central control, is for the provinces to appoint boards or committees of local citizens to advise provincial administrators. Neither of these methods, however, can achieve the co-ordination of local services and the responsiveness to local needs that is characteristic of direct administration by locally elected, general-purpose municipal Councils.

THE NEED FOR PROVINCIAL AID

The "Clear-cut" Theory

While most people agree that local government needs to be kept strong, there is quite a difference of opinion on how this can best be done. Some, in their enthusiasm for municipal autonomy, believe that the problem of centralization can be solved by adopting the "clear-cut" theory. The trouble, they say, is that the provinces have been meddling in too many of local government's affairs because there has been no clear-cut division between the functions of the local and provincial governments. All we need to do is create such a division by having the provinces take over entirely all services that have a wider-than-local aspect and leaving the municipalities in complete charge of the remainder. Then they would be free to run their own show, and local democracy would be kept strong.

To support their case the clear-cut theorists also bring in the benefit theory of taxation. They argue that local governments should not be paying for these wider-than-local services in any case, because revenues from the property tax, the main source of municipal revenue, should be used only to provide services that are of direct benefit to property — sidewalks, sewerage, fire protection, and so on. Hence the provinces should provide the services in such fields as welfare, health and education.

An objection to the benefit theory, however, is that it is almost impossible to distinguish between services that do and do not benefit property. As one writer has put it, to attempt to measure benefits is to engage in a "will-o'-the-wisp" search. Improved health and welfare in a neighbourhood, for example, may prevent it from developing into a slum and so lowering property values. And good schools certainly enhance the value of surrounding properties. In any case, the justification for a tax on property rests on other grounds: (1) real property is a tangible, inescapable evidence of wealth; (2) a uniform tax rate is a convenient way of requiring those who own more to pay more for services in which the whole community shares. Hence, as an argument against municipal administration of wider-than-local services, the benefit theory is fallacious. There is no good reason why municipal taxpayers should not be expected to pay at least a portion of the cost of such services.

But the major objection is to the clear-cut theory itself. While at first sight very attractive, it would provide no real solution to the problem of centralization simply because most of the important local services have taken on a wider-than-local aspect. If these were all taken over by the provinces, this would just be another big step in the direction of centralization. Local government would be left with very little to do. No useful purpose can be served by leaving municipalities free to rule their own domain if that domain includes nothing of any particular significance. Local government can be made strong only if it administers a significant proportion of all governmental services.

To meet these objections, some clear-cut theorists have an alternative proposal that looks even more attractive. If the municipalities have not been able to provide adequate social, educational and other services because of limited tax revenues, why not give them new sources of revenue? This would enable them to supply a wide range of these services entirely on their own and thus democracy could be kept at home. But the catch here is that if any of the provinces' major tax fields were handed over to the municipalities, the wealthy ones would collect far more than they needed while the poor ones still would be unable to provide adequate services. Besides, few of the taxes in these fields would be suitable for local collection. And of those that might be suitable, none could add significantly to total municipal revenues.

A New View

If we are to keep democracy at home, then, the question arises whether we should not take a new view of local government. In the old days local government had control over a limited number of fields. In these, it not only carried out policy but was free to decide what the policy was to be. Nowadays, however, because of the increasing interdependence of modern society, general policies must more and more be decided by the senior governments. Hence we must ask whether local government's function should not be, if not to pay for or decide major policy on wider-than-local services, at least to administer as large a number of these services as possible.

For example, suppose the local property tax can now support only about 20 per cent of the present-day cost of the social and educational services traditionally provided by municipalities. If local government were asked to pay the full cost of its services, it would be able to provide only 20 per cent of the services supplied in these fields. But suppose it were left, under appropriate general supervision, to perform nearly all of these services, and were asked to pay as its share only as much as the property tax can be expected to support. Then, since these services have expanded in recent years, the citizens participating in local government would be responsible for looking after even more services in their community than ever before. And local government would be consequently strengthened. Perhaps only in this way can local government maintain its position as the vehicle for grass-root participation in government. Otherwise it might be relegated to the position of providing only a small part of its traditional list of services.

This type of solution to the problem of centralization obviously requires a full-blown scheme of provincial aid. The provinces must look forward to paying for a generous share of the cost of municipally administered services. In oppositon to such a solution, the clear-cut theorists frequently argue that large grants from one level of government to another are bad, that they lead to irresponsibility. Since the spending authorities do not have to raise money the hard way—from the taxpayers — they are tempted to be extravagant, wasteful and even corrupt.

An examination of experience in many countries with grants of all kinds, however, leads to a serious questioning of this theory. Certainly the history of federal grants to the provinces — both general and conditional — does not confirm it. Nor does the experience so far with provincial aid. Before introducing its new provisions for the aged in 1951, the federal government for many years paid 75 per cent of the total cost of the joint old-age assistance scheme. And the provinces in some instances pay over 75 per cent of the total expenditure of local School Boards and up to 80 per cent for local welfare services. As an argument against a generous system of provincial aid, then, the theory should not be taken too seriously. The principle that a lower level of government should raise through taxation at least *some portion* of the total cost of the services it administers would seem to have a much firmer foundation in actual experience.

The Type of Aid

What type of provincial aid should be given? That the clear-cut theorists should dislike provincial aid, and regard it as a step toward centralization, is not surprising. So far the provinces have given aid mainly in the form of conditional grants for particular services. In effect they have said, "We will give you a grant of so much *provided* you supply such and such a service in such and such a way." Now this, of course, is a form of indirect control over the municipalities. True, they need not accept the grant. But if they do not they must do without the service, since they have not enough money of their own. Moreover, most conditional grants don't take adequate account of local differences in need. And because there has been no policy of over-all assistance, services aided by the provinces have prospered while other important municipal services have, relatively, starved.

At the same time, few would deny that provincial supervision of local services that are of wider-than-local interest is desirable. The provinces are legally superior to the municipalities and in the public interest have every right to control them directly if necessary. Conditional grants, then, are an excellent way of achieving supervision without direct control. It is much better to encourage local action with grants than to demand it legally. But this does not mean that all, or even most, provincial aid should be in the form of conditional grants.

When a province decides to aid its municipalities, however, the temptation to attach conditions is great. Ontario, for example, tried to meet the need for over-all assistance in 1949 by introducing a system whereby it shared the cost of a number of municipal services (the most important being police and fire). But the catch was that it paid only for specified services and only on expenditures which it approved. This meant close provincial supervision of important municipal services. The municipalities disliked the system so much that in 1953 it was revised, and the police and fire grants were abandoned.

After the war, only a few of the provinces were willing to experiment with full-blown schemes of general, unconditional aid. British Columbia and Alberta introduced systems of shared taxes whereby the municipalities received a portion of the revenues from certain provincial taxes — retail sales taxes and motor vehicle licence fees in British Columbia and fuel oil taxes in Alberta. The municipal shares were distributed mainly in proportion to the population in each municipality.[1] New Brunswick and Ontario also initiated grants of so many dollars per head of population, the amount per capita being larger for the urban units. In each case there were no strings attached and the municipalities were left free to spend the money in any way they saw fit. Thus the tendency of large-scale conditional grants to starve unaided services was at least partly offset, and the local units were enabled to provide more and better services with no loss of local autonomy.

The Problem of Equalization

A criticism of schemes such as these, however, is that they do not take adequate account of the tremendous differences between municipalities in their need for aid. Municipalities in poor areas find it much more difficult to raise money than do others. Hence their need for provincial aid is much greater. Moreover, many local units may have, in proportion to population, far more old people or children of school age for whom

[1] In Alberta, however, the share for rural municipalities was distributed one-third on a basis of need and two-thirds in proportion to each municipality's total rateable assessment. In B.C. the licence fee share had to be spent on roads.

they must supply costly services. Straight per capita grants, while better in this respect than most conditional grants and most tax-sharing schemes, do not go far enough toward equalizing these differences in both revenue-raising ability and need for services.

The British Columbia scheme made some allowance for differences in need for services since the grant from the sales tax took account of the school, as well as the total, population in a municipality. A further refinement might be to take account of the number of old people, too, since, besides children, they pay least taxes and use local health and welfare services most. This could be done by adjusting the population of a municipality for purposes of the per capita grant. If a municipality had more old people than average, its population figure would be increased proportionately. If it had fewer, the figure would be decreased.

To take account of differences in revenue-raising ability is, however, more difficult. The problem is to find a method of comparing the relative burden of taxation in each municipality. Some citizens and municipal officials falsely believe that comparing the height of the tax rate, or of taxes per ratepayer or per head, gives an indication. But the tax rate in particular may be quite misleading because of variations in standards of assessment. Municipalities whose assessments are at less than actual value have artificially high tax rates. In any case, what we want to know is not what the taxpayers in one municipality are *actually* paying relative to the others, but what they *can* pay. If the tax per head or per ratepayer in a municipality is high, one cannot necessarily say that the *burden* is great. Actually, expenditures and taxes may be high precisely because the citizens can *afford* better services. This partly explains why taxes are higher in the relatively wealthier urban municipalities. And this is why a system of aid which shares the cost of actual expenditures or which is distributed in direct proportion to assessed wealth, will favour the wealthy units.

How can one tell, then, whether a municipality is failing to provide average services because the tax burden would be too heavy or merely because it is shirking its duty in order to keep taxes low? The answer is that we must have some sort of index of its inhabitants' ability to pay local taxes. Ideally, taxable wealth per head would give us the comparison we want. And since most municipal taxes are based on property, taxable assessment per head comes close to this ideal. All a province would need to do to take account of differences in revenue-raising ability, then, would be to make a further adjustment in the population of a municipality for purposes of a per capita grant, according to the assessment. It would *reduce* the population figure where assessment per head was high and increase the figure where it was low. If real equalization is to be achieved, however, the standard of assessment throughout a province must be absolutely uniform. Otherwise, a municipality whose assessments were artificially low would get more than it deserved, and vice versa.[2]

Some people argue that granting provincial aid on a fully equalized basis would result in such a complicated formula that local officials would not understand it. It would require so many adjustments to the basic grants that some municipalities could easily become convinced they were not being treated fairly. But if the aid were in the form of general per capita grants and the adjustments were objective and scientific, using only a few basic indexes of need, as suggested, this should not be a problem. Britain has had such a scheme since 1929, and there is general agreement among her local units that it has worked successfully.

THE NEED FOR LARGER UNITS

The solution to the problem of centralization proposed here — that local government should be enabled through provincial aid to administer more services — has one major objection. At the present time it would not provide as efficient a system of administration as would the by-passing of municipal government in favour of the provinces.

The main reason for this is that a great many of the local authorities are too small and financially weak to administer an expanded load of services efficiently — even with generous provincial aid on an equalized basis. Small units cannot provide the specialized knowledge, equipment and personnel needed for the efficient administration of modern social services. Experts tell us that for this purpose a municipality should have at least 30,000 inhabitants, and ideally should have upwards of 50,000. Yet only the larger cities and a few suburban municipalities meet this requirement. Statistics for 1971 show that the average population of the more than 4,000 local governments in Canada (excluding the second-tier units) is only about 4,800. The large cities pull up this average, and the

[2] For this reason, if large-scale provincial aid is to be based partly on assessment, or on the cost of a service above a uniform tax rate, as with several provincial schemes for education, assessing should probably become a provincial function.

vast majority of municipalities actually have populations below 4,800.

Since municipal organization varies from province to province, the local units in some provinces are, on the average, much smaller than in others. The approximate average population of the unitary municipalities in each province is shown in the following tabulation:[3]

Newfoundland 3,400
Prince Edward Island 2,300
Nova Scotia 12,100
New Brunswick 3,500
Quebec 3,600
Ontario 8,800
Manitoba 5,300
Saskatchewan 1,200
Alberta 4,900
British Columbia 14,900
CANADA 4,800

Saskatchewan has by far the smallest units, with a municipality for every 1,200 people. Those in Quebec, New Brunswick and P.E.I. are also relatively small, their average populations being considerably less than 4,000. The largest units are in Nova Scotia and British Columbia. But even here the averages are under 15,000 persons per municipality. Thus there is no province in Canada in which the basic units of local government are on the average big enough to provide for large-scale operation.

In 1966 New Brunswick's government took a drastic step to meet this problem, as well as the earlier ones we have been discussing. It simply abolished all of the province's rural municipalities and took over — not only from them but also from the urban units — all services that required large-scale operation. These included assessment, justice, health, welfare and education (though the latter is administered in large school

---

[3] Based on 1971 census figures for provincial populations, decreased by an estimate of the population living outside the municipalities in each province. For the three provinces without rural municipalities (Newfoundland, Prince Edward Island and New Brunswick), the averages are only approximate, calculated by estimating the rural population to be about a third of the total.

districts by boards having a majority of elected members). This action was mainly prompted by the desire to raise the standard of such services in the poor, French-speaking areas of the province. But the question is whether this could not have been done by other means, without centralization and the abolition of local government.

If citizens and local authorities are genuinely interested in preserving and strengthening local control, they must give serious consideration to this question. What is needed to meet the challenge of the greater technical efficiency of central administration is larger units of local government. One cannot expect citizens to endure patiently the unequal, inefficient or non-supplying of important social services merely for the sake of the theoretical and intangible objective of keeping democracy at home. Nor is it right to use provincial aid as a device for perpetuating small and inefficient local units.

To abolish all small municipalities in order to put large ones in their place would, of course, be much too drastic a solution. It would involve snuffing out the flames of self-government and community spirit in hundreds of small towns and villages across the country, and would thus be a form of centralization just as serious as having the provinces take over all wider-than-local services. This objection does not apply with the same force, however, to the enlargement of rural municipalities, since they are usually not clearly defined communities in any case. Yet rural citizens and officials are so notorious for their adherence to tradition that the abolition of existing rural units would probably be strenuously opposed. So far, Alberta is the only province that has succeeded in enlarging its rural municipalities. This was done by combining the old units rather than directly abolishing them. As a result, the new ones are only a little more than twice as large as the old ones and, in terms of population, are still relatively small.

Proposed Municipal Regions

Fortunately, there is a solution to the problem of size which involves neither the abolition nor the combining of existing municipalities. And that is to create enlarged units, governed by locally appointed or elected Councils, to administer only those services that require large areas for efficient administration. With such a scheme it would not be necessary to uproot the existing municipal institutions. Instead, a second tier of regional governments would be created which would contain the existing local units. These governments would administer only municipal services of wider-than-local interest (such as health, welfare, institutional care, education, and secondary roads). But they could also administer provincial services capable of being provided by municipal authorities on a regional basis. Taxes to pay the local share of the cost of all these services would then be levied at a uniform rate over a whole region, thus equalizing the burden. This is the sort of concession local authorities must be prepared to make to the growing interdependence of modern society if the double objective of strengthening local government and providing more efficient services is to be achieved.

A scheme such as this was proposed by the author in 1949 for Nova Scotia, including the Halifax metropolitan area, in a report on the reorganization of provincial-municipal relations in that province. Ontario and Quebec already have the skeleton for such a system in their Counties. These large units have average populations of about 60,000 in Ontario and 20,000 in Quebec, and are governed by representatives from the municipalities which they contain. But in both provinces the Counties exclude cities, some of which are small. Quebec's Counties also exclude towns, most of which are very small. And in neither province do the County governments have many functions. If they were reorganized and stream-lined, however, they could be made to carry a much heavier load of wider-than-local services.

A recent move in this direction has been the creation of second-tier governments in the main metropolitan areas of Ontario and Quebec. Like the County governments, their Councils are composed of members from the local Councils, but their powers and functions are much greater. The Ontario government has now found it possible to decentralize a number of provincial functions to these new units. Their success may well provide a pattern for the province-wide reorganization of local government generally in Canada.

Some provinces, such as Nova Scotia, have already found it necessary to decentralize many of their provincial health, welfare, and other services into regions. Hence, many of these services could easily be placed under the control of locally elected regional authorities. Other provinces, like Saskatchewan, have created enlarged local districts for such things as health, hospitals and education. But these districts do not coincide and each service is under a separate authority. It would seem logical, for the sake of co-ordination and efficiency, to tie the boundaries of such divisions together into municipal regions, and to place the services under the control of the same set of elected officials — the regional Council. In recent years Alberta has tied together most of its rural School and Municipal Districts into so-called Counties. There seems no good reason why a similar co-ordination of services in much larger areas, which would include both rural and urban units, should not be successful.

So far, British Columbia is the only province that has introduced a province-wide system of regional governments such as we have proposed. Though these governments have not yet been delegated many powers, they have the potential to take over additional powers and services, not only from the local level but also from the province, thus reversing the centralizing trend and keeping democracy closer to home.

Attaining the Objective

If the nation-wide need for larger municipal units were to be met in the way suggested, there seems little doubt that the objective of a strong, efficient local government structure would be attained — and democracy could be kept at home. Able, imaginative persons would be much more likely to run for election or to become local officials if they knew that they would not be frustrated in everything they tried to do by institutions which no longer meet the needs of modern society. Even more important, citizens would take much more interest in local government if they knew it had an important job to do. Those who complain about the decline of interest in municipal affairs often fail to observe that local authorities are not being left with tasks that can captivate the citizens' interest.

If for the sake of efficiency the main social functions of government are transferred to the provinces, a valuable aspect of democratic government will be lost. It is questionable whether technical efficiency should be the overriding consideration. Higher values are at stake. Municipal provision of services is one of the most effective ways of ensuring that government action is kept under the control of the citizens and made responsive to their local needs. It also develops leadership and prepares local talent for work in a wider field. To strengthen local government in the way suggested, then, would be to strengthen democracy.

But how can a reorganization such as that proposed be brought about?

We in this country are fortunate in having a system of government where such a reorganization is quite possible, provided there is sufficient public recognition of the need. The people of the United States, in comparison, are not as fortunate. In some American states the structure of local government is frozen so rigidly into the state Constitution that it cannot be melted free; in others, no agreement can be reached as to who should be responsible for reorganization. But in this country the structure of local government is the creation of provincial Legislatures, and a provincial Cabinet can assume the leadership and responsibility necessary to carry through a reorganization.

Naturally, however, provincial governments do not wish to give away any of their powers unless they feel this to be absolutely necessary. In fact, they are tempted by the need for efficiency to do just the reverse. Hence they are not likely to embark upon a far-reaching programme to strengthen local government unless pressed by citizens who have discussed the problem enough to know—at least in a general way—what needs to be done.

Wide-Awake Public Discussion

The achievement of such a reorganization does not mean that the problem of centralization will be completely solved. If citizens are to ensure that this more efficient, but more remote and complex, organization of local government is responsive to their needs, they must keep a firm grip on the controls. They must determine generally *what* is to be done through influencing their elected representatives, and also *how* it is to be done through advising their public officials. In order to do this they must engage in vigorous democratic discussion and make their views known. More and more we are coming to realize that it is not only the number of citizens actually sitting on Councils and other local bodies that is important, but also the number who are actively keeping track of what these bodies and their officials are doing.

With so many competing interests in modern society, however, citizens can't be expected to take a really active interest in municipal affairs unless directly encouraged to do so. Yet there is hardly a municipality in Canada that has a programme for informing its citizens about civic affairs, to say nothing of otherwise stimulating their interest in local problems. It is true that most municipalities publish annual financial reports. But little attempt is made to distribute them widely. In any case, it would take a qualified accountant to interpret them intelligently. How many of them can be understood by Mr. John Q. Citizen—the man who should know because he's paying the bills? Clearly, if John Q.'s interest in local government is to be stimulated, municipalities must foster well-organized programmes of education and discussion about municipal affairs.

It cannot be emphasized too strongly that the cure for a sleepy public is wide-awake public discussion. The complete solution to the problem of centralization will not be attained until local citizens become keenly interested in local affairs.

For Further Reading

If you are interested in learning more about local government in general, or in delving more deeply into some of the special topics covered, you may wish to take a look at some of the following suggested readings. An effort has been made to select materials that would be of interest to the lay reader and at the same time are readily available from a local library or bookstore, or can be ordered by a bookstore from the publishers. Hence, articles in periodicals have been omitted.

The list has been completely revised for the second edition, and consists mainly of very recent publications. Where necessary, brief annotations indicate the contents, and in most cases the number of pages is given, especially if the publication is only a short one, such as a brochure or pamphlet.

General Readings

Crawford, K. G. *Canadian Municipal Government.* Toronto: University of Toronto Press, 1954. 407 pp. Old but comprehensive.

Feldman, Lionel D., and Michael Goldrick, eds. *Politics and Government of Urban Canada: Selected Readings.* Toronto: Methuen, 1969; 2nd ed. 1972. 433 pp.

Humes, Samuel, and E.M. Martin. *The Structure of Local Government: A Comparative Survey.* The Hague: International Union of Local Authorities, 1969. Covers 81 countries.

Krueger, Ralph R., and Charles Bryfogle, eds. *Urban Problems: a Canadian Reader.* Toronto: Holt, Rinehart and Winston, 1971.

Plunkett, Thomas J. *Urban Canada and Its Government.* Toronto: Macmillan, 1968. 178 pp.

Robson, William A., and D. E. Regan, eds. *Great Cities of the World: Their Government, Politics and Planning.* 2 vols. London: Allen & Unwin, 3rd ed. 1972. Includes Montreal and Toronto.

Rowat, Donald C. *The Canadian Municipal System: Essays on the Improvement of Local Government.* Toronto: McClelland and Stewart, 1969. 242 pp. Has an extensive bibliography.

Statistics Canada. *Canada Year Book.* Ottawa: Information Canada. See latest edition, chapter on Constitution and Government, section on Local Government, for basic recent information.

Readings on Special Topics

Adler, Gerald M. *Land Planning by Administrative Regulation: the Policies of the Ontario Municipal Board.* Toronto: University of Toronto Press, 1971. 246 pp.

Axworthy, Lloyd, and J. M. Gillies, eds. *The City: Canada's Prospects, Canada's Problems.* Toronto: Butterworths, 1973.

Bureau of Municipal Research. *Reorganizing Local Government — A Brief Look at Four Provinces.* Toronto: Civic Affairs, No. 1, 1972. 31 pp. British Columbia, Alberta, Ontario and New Brunswick.

Cameron, David M. *Schools for Ontario.* Toronto: University of Toronto Press, 1972. 331 pp.

Clarkson, Stephen. *City Lib: Parties and Reform in Toronto.* Toronto: Hakkert, 1972.

Connor, Des. *Citizens Participate: An Action Guide for Public Issues.* Oakville: Development Press, 1975. 64 pp.

Draper, James A., ed. *Citizen Participation: Canada.* Toronto: New Press, 1971.

Fraser, Graham. *Fighting Back: Urban Renewal in Trefann Court.* Toronto: Hakkert, 1972. 298 pp.

Granatstein, J. L. *Marlborough Marathon.* Toronto: James Lewis and Samuel, 1971. Residents fight a development proposal in Toronto.

Hickey, Paul. *Decision-Making Processes in Ontario's Local Governments.* Toronto: Information Canada, 1973. 501 pp. Makes proposals for reform.

Kaplan, Harold. *The Regional City: Politics and Planning in Metropolitan Areas.* Toronto: Canadian Broadcasting Corporation, 1965. 55 pp.

Lawless, Henry Alan, ed. *The Politics of Government Finance.* Ottawa: Canadian Federation of Mayors and Municipalities, 1969. 117 pp.

Lithwick, N. Harvey. *Urban Canada: Problems and Prospects*. Ottawa: CMHC, 1970. Proposes a federal policy on urban development.

Lorimer, James. *A Citizen's Guide to City Politics*. Toronto: James Lewis and Samuel, 1972. 216 pp. Argues that developers control city halls.

Lorimer, James. *The Real World of City Politics*. Toronto: James Lewis and Samuel, 1970.

Masson, Jack K., and D. Anderson, eds. *Emerging Politics in Urban Canada*. Toronto: McClelland and Stewart, 1973. Readings.

Ontario Economic Council. *Municipal Reform: a Proposal for the Future*. Toronto: Information Canada, 1971.

Ontario Economic Council. *Subject to Approval*. Toronto: Information Canada, 1973. Municipal planning in Ontario.

Plunkett, Thomas J. *Winnipeg: Canada's Third Largest City, an Explanation of Its New Government*. Winnipeg: City of Winnipeg, 1972.

Powell, Alan, ed. *The City: Attacking Modern Myths*. Toronto: McClelland and Stewart, 1972. 271 pp. Essays on solutions to urban problems.

Price, T., ed. *Regional Government in Ontario*. Don Mills: Science Research Associates, 1971.

Richardson, Boyce. *The Future of Canadian Cities*. Toronto: New Press, 1972. 259 pp. Proposes solutions to urban problems.

Rose, Albert. *Governing Metropolitan Toronto*. Berkeley: University of California Press, 1973. 201 pp.

Sewell, John. *Up Against City Hall*. Toronto: James Lewis and Samuel, 1972. 224 pp.

Bibliographies

Grasham, W. E., comp. *Canadian Public Administration Bibiography.* Toronto: Institute of Public Administration of Canada, 1972, and Supplement 1, 1974. Has a long municipal section.

Urban and Regional References 1945-1969. Ottawa: Canadian Council on Urban and Regional Research, 1971, and Supplement 1971, 1972. Lists over 7,000 items on urban affairs.

Index

Accounting methods, 76, 90, 91
Acts, municipal. *See* Provincial legislation
Alberta: provision for local government in, 11–12; legislation governing cities in, 17; number of municipalities in, 18, 19; Board of Commissioners system in, 26; health services in, 96; enlargement of rural units in, 97, 114; grants in, 110; size of municipalities in, 113; new Counties in, 116. *See also* Western provinces
Aldermen, 24, 27
American Revolution, influence of, 5–6
Arbitration, boards of, 92
Assessment, fixed, 80–81; procedure, 81–82; standards, 82–83, 111, 112; appeals, 83; being taken over by provinces, 83; equalization of, 83, 112

Board of Commissioners system, 26
Board of Control system in Ontario, 26–27

Boards: of Police, 7; nature of, 43–44; to operate municipal utilities, 57; of arbitration, 92; *See also* Health Boards, Ontario Municipal Board, School Boards
Borrowing, voter approval of, 34, 44; provincial supervision of, 48, 86, 87, 90–91; methods of, 85–86; timing of, 87–88
British Columbia: provision for local government in, 11–12; number of municipalities in, 18, 19; exemption of improvements in, 80; hospital insurance in, 95; grants in, 100, 110, 111; size of municipalities in, 113. *See also* Western provinces
Budget, municipal, 84
Business taxes, revenues from, 74, 75; types of, 78–79
By-laws, 34, 38, 43; nature of, 46; how passed, 46–47; provincial approval of, 47–49, 91–92; quashing of, 49

Cabinet system, 26; for local governments, 29–31

Capital expenditures, methods of financing, 76, 85—87; timing of, 87—88

Charts: number of municipalities, 19

City governments: provision for in Upper and Lower Canada, 7; in Western Canada, 10—12; legislation governing, 16—17; populations for, 17; number of, 17, 18; size of Councils in, 25; forms of, 25—31; payment of Councillors in, 39—40; powers of Mayor in, 42; utilities owned by, 56—57; Planning Boards of, 59

City Manager. *See* Manager plan

Clerk-Treasurer, 64; as Manager, 67

Commissioners. *See* Board of Commissioners

Commissions, nature of, 43—44; to operate utilities, 57, 76

Committees of Council, 43—45, 66—67

Councils, municipal: nature of, 22, 24—25, 26—29 *pass.*; how elected, 23—24; size of, 25; payment of members of, 39—40; meetings of, 42; procedure and organization of, 42—45, 66—67; powers of, 53—58, 62, 80—81, 83; planning role of, 58—59, 60; expenditures of, 60—61; revenues of, 73—76; financing by, 76, 84—88 *pass.*

County governments: origin of, 8—10; influence of, 11—12; chairman in, 14, 23; nature of, 16—17, 20; number of, 18, 19; functions of, 20; size of Councils in, 25; tax levies of, 82; as regional units, 97, 115; size of, 115

Courts, may question by-laws, 48—49; municipal functions of, 48—49, 50, 83, 85, 91; may hold municipality liable, 50; appeal on dismissal to, 64; nature of lower, 69—72; appeal on assessment to, 83; tax warrant of, 85; arbitration by, 91. *See also* Justice

Courts of Quarter Sessions, 2—3, 6—9 *pass.*, 13

Debt, interest on, 60—61, 86—88 *pass.*; provision for repayment of, 60—61, 76, 86—87; total municipal, 87; reduction of, 103—104

Departmental organization, municipal, 66—67

Departments of Municipal Affairs, 67, 89—92 *pass. See also* Provincial supervision

Districts, special. *See* Regional units

Education, provincial-local responsibility for, 54—55, 93—95; municipal expenditures for, 60—61, 94; grants for, 93, 94; federal responsibility for, 93; Departments of, 93, 95. *See also* School Boards

Election campaign, 39

Employment rules, 68—69

Equalization, of assessments, 82, 111—112; of tax burden, 102, 111—112; of services, 111

Executive Committee system in

Montreal and Quebec, 27–29
Executive Council, irresponsible rule by, 8
Exemptions from taxation, 79–81
Expenditures, municipal, 60–61, 103, 104

Form of local government: Mayor-Council, 23–24; Council-Manager, 25–26, 28, 45, 78; Board of Commissioners, 26; Board of Control, 26–27; Executive Committee, 27–29; possible Cabinet, 29

General vote, election by: of Council head, 23; of Councillors, 24; of Controllers, 27
Grand Jury, 2–4 pass., 8

Halifax: granted self-government, 8; Manager plan in, 26; Mayor in, 14; business and household taxes in, 78; real property tax in, 79; metropolitan area, 115
Hamilton, size of Council in, 25; city government in, 26–27
Head of Council: of local municipality sits on County Council, 16; nature of, 23–24, 25–28 pass.; how chosen, 23–24; name of, 23; powers of, 42
Health, provincial-local responsibility for, 57, 95–97, 100; municipal expenditures for, 60–61, 100; Boards, 96–97; officers, 97; federal responsibility for, 97–98; insurance, 95–96
Home and School Associations, 95
Household tax, 78

Howe, Joseph, 8

Incorporation, meaning of, 50

Judges, 70–72 pass.
Justice, administration of: municipal cost of, 54, 72, 74; nature of lower Courts, 69–72; by provinces, 92. See also Courts
Justices of the Peace, former functions of, 2–4, 6, 7, 8; present functions of, 71

Kingston, 7

Labour relations, 68–69, 91–92
Laws. See Provincial legislation
Liability, legal, of municipalities, 50–51
Licences, permits, etc., 74, 75
Loans, provincial, 87, 94
Local Improvement Districts, 15
London, 7
Loyalist immigration, 6–7

Magistrates, 70, 71
Manager plan, 25–26, 28, 45
Manitoba: provision for local government in, 10–11; municipal legislation in, 17; number of municipalities in, 19; business tax in, 78; size of municipalities in, 113. See also Western provinces
Maritime provinces: influx of Loyalists into, 6–7; poll tax in, 76; personal property tax in, 78; roads in, 55, 92; provision for the poor in, 98–99
Mayor. See Head of Council
Mayor-Council system, 23–24

Meetings of Council, 42, 45, 51
Metropolitan government: problem of, 20—21; provisions for, 21; Toronto, 21, 25, 115; proposed Halifax, 115
Ministers of Municipal Affairs, 47—49, 90—92 *pass. See also* Provincial supervision
Money by-laws, vote on, 34, 38; provincial approval of, 47, 90
Montreal: granted self-government, 7; metropolitan Protestant School Board, 21; Metropolitan Commission, 21; size of Council in, 25; city government in, 27—29; population of, 29; proportion voting in, 33; number of civic employees in, 68

New Brunswick: as separate colony, 6; provision for local government in, 9; rural-urban co-operation in, 18—19; number of municipalities in, 19; roads in, 55; the poor in, 98—99; grants in, 110; size of municipalities in, 113. *See also* Maritime provinces
Newfoundland: provision for local government in, 9, 15; number of municipalities in, 19; supervision of municipalities in, 91; health services in, 95; size of municipalities in, 113
Nomination procedure, 38—39
Nova Scotia: provision for local government in, 8, 9, 15; granted responsible government, 8; rural-urban co-operation in, 18—19; number of munici-

palities in, 19; qualifications for Councillors in, 37; approval of by-laws in, 47, 91; roads in, 55, 92; tax exemptions in, 94; tax collection in, 80; hospitals in, 95; Health Divisions in, 97; the poor in, 98—99; size of municipalities in, 113; proposed regions in, 115. *See also* Maritime provinces
Numbers of municipalities, by type and province, 19; of persons per municipality, 112, 113

Ontario: provision for local government in, 7, 9—10; County government in, 14, 16—17, 18, 19, 20, 23, 25, 115; population for cities and towns in, 17; number of municipalities in, 18, 19; Board of Control system in, 26—27; Council head's vote in, 42; business tax in, 78; grants in, 94, 110; assessment appeals in, 83; approval of by-laws in, 91; Health Units in, 97; size of municipalities in, 113, 115
Ontario Municipal Board, 47, 83, 91
Ordinances, 46—49
Ottawa, incorporated, 7; size of Council in, 25; city government in, 26—27; annexations, 21, 25

Parish governments, origins of, 5; provision for in Lower Canada, 10; method of election in, 25
Parties, political, in local elections, 30, 31
Payment, of Councillors, 39—40; of civic employees, 68—69, 91;

Voting procedure, 34–36, 39

Wards, 23, 24, 25, 27, 28
Welfare, provincial-local responsibility for, 54–55, 57, 95,
97–100; municipal expenditures for, 60–61, 100; federal
responsibility for, 97–98;
grants for, 100
Western provinces: regional districts in, 20, 22, 95, 97, 100,
115–116; income from utilities
in, 75, 80; exemption of improvements in, 80; provincial
valuation in, 83; assessment appeals in, 83; Departments of
Municipal Affairs in, 89; health
services in, 95, 96; Health Units
in, 97
Winnipeg, granted self-government, 11; metropolitan districts,
21; size of Council in, 25

Zoning, 58, 59–60 *pass.*